BIGFOOT
TERROR IN THE WOODS

Sightings and Encounters / vol. 1

by William J. Sheehan

Whether or not Bigfoot is real or imagined is something that is yet to be determined. Therefore this book is a work of fiction. Names, characters, locations and incidents are either the results of the interviewees imaginations, or if they are true, have not been proven to be so. Any resemblance to actual people be they living or dead, or any events of any kind is purely coincidental in nature.

Copyright © 2019 William J. Sheehan

All rights reserved.

ISBN: 978-1717211941

If you've seen something, say something.

Email splinters@optonline.net

For media inquiries contact splinters@optonline.net

Cover and text design by Casey Smith, hello@sugarstudiosdesign.com

Introduction

As I begin to spin these tales into what I believe will be the making of something comprehensible out of the incomprehensible. A brief but necessary introduction of myself is in order. Firstly may I say that I personally have never seen a Bigfoot. And I have never been deeper into the forest than the Pine Barrens on Long Island. Or perhaps in my youth on some camping excursions with the Boy Scouts or my family in the states of Vermont, New Hampshire and New York. As a young boy my father nicknamed me eagle eye. He was a pilot and as a hobbyist he was one of the very first involved in radio control airplanes. During my time with my dad I became fairly adept at shall we say finding a needle in a haystack. Small pieces would occasionally fall or vibrate loose from his planes in the sky. And I had an uncanny ability to scour an open field and find them. I was also very good at finding planes in the woods when the radio failed. The plane now flying out of control into the distant trees. My father was a reasonably intelligent man and in fact maybe more so.

He was a weather observer for the F.A.A. and had a vast knowledge of aircraft, trains, weather and the sky in general.

He also had a good working knowledge as well of all things mechanical having been an aircraft mechanic in New Guinea during the war. So why do I begin by mentioning all of this you may be saying to yourself? In particular when I am beginning a book on the elusive Sasquatch. The fact is that as I grew I took on many of the traits of my dad and then some. I could identify every plane in the sky be they commercial, recreational or military. I was a sky and star gazer. He and I would look for and identify constellations, planets and the like. I knew and could identify all cloud formations on any given day of the week. And I had become an avid bird watcher. To this very day I spend a good deal of time seeking out and identifying new birds in my area. The newest being a Snowy Owl seen in Hampton Bays just a few nights ago. A bird which I spotted sitting by the marshes edge on Fire Island. I am a Catholic Christian author and blogger. And for any who may be interested my blog is THEPROPHETICPUNDIT. COM. I am also an avid fisherman, trap and skeet shooter. And I have as of late thrown my hat into the ring so to speak. With the purchase of several old recurve bows going headlong into the sport of archery.

In my life I have found that most people live like an ostrich with their heads buried in the ground. They see nothing because their eyes and senses are not conditioned to see. And this is caused primarily in my opinion from a lack of use. I have personally had many experiences with angels. And have twice had my life saved by one. Because of this I know what it is to tell someone in earnest about what I have seen or experienced. Only to have them roll their eyes in disbelief and quickly change the subject. As if what I had just said to them had no merit whatsoever. Nevertheless I know what I have seen and experienced. I see and understand simply because I am looking and seeking. And so do many of you. You were not with my wife and me the other night when we drove over the bridge crossing the Great South Bay. As we spotted the Snowy Owl sitting on a street sign by the marsh. And yet it was there and so were we. My wife and I have been together now for some 25 years. During our time together she has been continually amazed at my ability to spot hawks and owls sitting in trees. And to point out deer lurking in the shadows. Deer that she previously had no knowledge even existed. And over time I have taught her how to better see them for herself as well as teaching her some of my own techniques for doing so.

And so why do I say all of this to you? In a nutshell I know what I am looking at. And I am well skilled in the act of observation. It is part of my DNA. I am curious about all things. By the mouth of a single witness and with perhaps the presence of some circumstantial evidence. Men have been sentenced to imprisonment and even death. And some for crimes they did not commit. And yet we have avid woodsmen. Experienced hikers and mountaineers. People who know uninhabited forests like their own backyard. Men and women who live their lives and or make their livelihoods in the woods of North America. Fisherman, loggers and the like who have seen and experienced things that were so fearful and horrific in nature that they were afraid to speak of them. Some have lost friends and loved ones in deadly encounters. Only to have them shrugged off as bear attacks and missing person accounts. They have been lied about and ridiculed. And all of this while they stood their ground telling the truth as to what happened to them in the woods that fateful day. False reports have been filed. And bogus news stories have been spoken and printed. Twisting the truth of what really happened to them on the day of their encounter.

And so as not to be long winded in my preparations to write. I have said enough about me. My intent is this. That in a relatively brief and concise fashion. And perhaps in the form of a number of short volumes. I will endeavor to put down on paper some of the most intense and horrifying encounters which I have received to date. Encounters with the beast known as Bigfoot. Encounters and sightings that have occurred in the woods and parks of our North American continent. And many other accounts which involved no sighting of the beast whatsoever. Where we are left with mere circumstantial evidence. Scratching our heads if you will as to what did or did not happen at the scene of the incident. Together you and I will review the evidence for ourselves as it is presented by the people who were there. And now momentarily allow me to give you a little insight into just how I personally apply my powers of observation and intuition. Which will then give you a window into how I make my own judgements as they pertain to the stories you will read. And the testimonies which you will be privy to.

Let's just say for a moment that I am riding down the street in my truck. And to the right of me on the side of the road I see a fire hydrant lying on its side. Apparently having been disconnected from its mount. Which one can reasonably assume it was previously connected to. Now call me stupid but my first thought is this. At some point prior to my seeing it this hydrant was hit by a car. A car that is no longer there for me to see. Are you with me so far? Now if you can or will not buy into the scenario which I have just put forth. You and I must then engage in just what else could have happened which rendered the hydrant lying on the side of the road. And so getting out of the truck and moving in for a closer look at the scene. We now observe not only the hydrant. But we can now clearly see that the pipe to which it was affixed has been snapped off. Reinforcing my presumption that an impact or force of some kind had occurred shearing the hydrant from its mount.

In other words it was not unbolted maliciously by some vandal. It is becoming more obvious to the eye that a vehicle or device of some kind must have impacted the hydrant with great force. Enough force to snap the cast iron piping sending the hydrant flying down the roadside. And in reality what else can or could we say? Perhaps that some behemoth walked by grabbing the hydrant with the strength of an elephant breaking it free from its mounts. This would however be utter nonsense. The point being made is nothing more than this. You and I know based on even the simplest forms of evidence and having been given certain criteria. That we have a God given ability to make a reasonable assumption. An assumption as to what has happened and what has not happened when we both see and observe certain things. It doesn't require a crime scene investigation team to interpret the information to me and or for me. As to what did and did not happen to the fire hydrant. And it is in this same light of reasoning that I believe you and I together can and will come to the same conclusions. As to what did and did not happen to these individuals as they tell their own stories in their own way.

I will not in any way openly identify the individuals whose testimonies you will read by using their real names. I will as well in many of the stories alter precise locations by giving the reader more generalized locations of the events. Be they regional, state by state or in some cases using the names of parks, wetlands, mountainous regions or other locational hints. This I will do in an effort to narrow down the playing field in the mind's eye. The reality being this. For many of you these sightings and encounters are occurring with regularity in your state and in your county. And if I was to name your street and town as being the location you would more than likely say that it was rubbish. Or if I was to speak of the park which is a half hour ride from your home as being the scene of an encounter. You would likely also say how can that be? I have been hiking there my entire life and have seen nothing of the sort.

To me the cold hard facts are these as they relate to the human condition. People for the most part live sheltered and protected lives in our country. They are far removed from any sense of danger or devastating mishaps potentially occurring in their lives. For instance most people do not ponder for one split second. Or give any credence to the notion that the boat in which they go fishing every week is going to sink the next time they go out. We don't give it a moment's thought. Or that this very morning on the way to work the crossing gate will not come down in a torrential rain storm. And a train will impact their car. As I stated earlier I have had some mind boggling events happen in my life. They were not and could not be planned for. They came out of nowhere and ended as quickly as they began. Leaving me as the only living witness to what had happened. And so it is that I myself believe in Bigfoot having never seen one. And I believe as well that normal God fearing human beings. Honest everyday hard working individuals. Have in the course of their daily lives encountered the dreadful and the unthinkable. Some have come across bloodied corpses and have been attacked and in fear of their very lives. They have encountered the terror in the woods. Bigfoot! As you read these accounts I will be writing from the viewpoint of the party who was interviewed. I will not be trying to impress you in any way with my writing skills. And I will promise you that due diligence will be given in the hope of ensuring that each and every account is as accurate as they were presented to me by the individuals who told them.

Contents

17 | The Michigan Upper Peninsula Encounter

33 | The Shenandoah Park Sighting

41 | The Fitzpatrick Wilderness Sighting

51 | The Rock Hounds Encounter

63 | The Vancouver Evidence

71 | The Great Divide Trail Encounter

79 | The Yellowstone Scouting Encounter

85 | The Stone Mountain Sighting

93 | The Strawberry Lake Trail 5 Encounter

99 | Missing Person Washington State

105 | The Over Mountain Victory Trail Encounter

111 | The Mars Hill Incident

119 | The Loggers Tale

123 | The 1939 Cheyenne Mountain Sighting

129 | The Merced River Sighting

135 | The Prospectors Letter

141 | The Manitoba Evidence

147 | He Must Have Run Away

153 | The Deer Feeder Evidence

161 | The Fire Jumper

167 | The Hobo Camps

171 | Highway Patrol

175 | The Helenbar Lookout Trail Sighting

183 | The Rutland County Sighting

191 | The Wagon Train Diary

193 | The New Brunswick Account

195 | The Travelers Diary

199 | The Fur Trappers Evidence

207 | The Medora Monster

213 | The Howler

217 | The Pheasant Hunters

223 | The Green House Evidence

231 | Ziggy Stardust

243 | The Troopers Tale

249 | No Bull

255 | The South Carolina Incident

265 | The Roosevelt Elk Encounter

273 | The Prairie Creek Redwoods State Park Sighting

279 | The Dead Falls Lake Affair

287 | The Black Bear Incident

295 | The Turkey Hunters Sighting

301 | The Shape Shifter Encounter

The Michigan Upper Peninsula Encounter

Pat Sullivan and Aarto Raikonen had first made their acquaintance during a boot camp stint at Paris Island. Having both set their minds on joining the U.S.M.C. in 1979.

From here on out it is from Patrick's recollection that the story will move forward. I told you already that Artie and I met during boot camp. By the way his real name is Aarto which he told me in Finnish means bear man. And having mentioned him being Finnish I thought it rather remarkable that his entire family was of pure Finnish heritage. Even more remarkable to me was that all of the family had migrated at the same time to the United States in the late 1800s. All of whom live together in the Upper Peninsula of Michigan in Alger county.

During boot Artie and I hit it off well. And whenever we could get a moment to sit and talk we did. I learned over time that he and I had quite allot in common. We both fished and we both liked to shoot. The two of us also had a great love for the outdoors. And so it was that during this time in the service he and I had both agreed to visit each other on our home turf after the military gig was finished. He however was a hunter and I had never hunted per say. But rather had spent my time shooting sporting clays.

In the summer of 1985 I packed up my truck and headed to Arties house in Michigan. One of the things which I had packed was my 12 gauge semi auto Berretta. Which Artie had advised would be needed for protection. When I asked him the question exactly what are we protecting ourselves from? He said bears. Fair enough I said to myself. So now I knew that there were bears where Artie lived and I wondered as well what else may be living there.

I spent two days cruising up into his neck of the woods. And when I starting getting close woods it was. This place was to me like the forest primeval. I mean gravel and dirt roads surrounded by thick predominantly pine forests with an occasional sighting of a house or building. After having been turned around numerous times in my effort to find his house. In other words I was lost. I finally thank God found their hacienda.

It was quite the spread consisting of a large house and a smaller one that were surrounded by a number of barns and out buildings. So I pulled into the driveway and hit the horn. And suddenly it was as if I was in the middle of a family reunion. People were springing out of everywhere both young and old. They were greeting me as if I was the prodigal son returning home. I said to myself that this was going to be a great time. After the initial meet and greet I was given the nickel tour of the homestead. One of the barns was like a machine shop slash blacksmith shop.

These dudes had everything. Apparently great grandpa made allot of the metal tools and goods back in the day both for himself and the surrounding residents. In one of the other barns when the door was opened. It was loaded with professional lumber yard and milling equipment. As it turns out his family had actually created from the surrounding forest much of what their home and the homes of many other families in the area were made out of.

These folks were made from the real stock. They knew what to do and how to do it and they were proud of it. As the day continued into night Artie had put together quite a criteria for the next nine days. His plan was for us to tour around and see the surrounding sights. Followed by some camping, hiking and fishing in the truest sense of wilderness style. It all sounded great to me.

After dinner had been prepared and eaten. Which by the way was served up like Thanksgiving. His father had taken me into the den in order to peruse the family's gun collection. In this den they had three gun cabinets. Each ones wood having aged differently and one being more beautiful than the next. The three having been hand crafted as the collection grew through the years. They had forty seven rifles and shotguns. And the draws beneath the cabinets were stocked with hand guns. These were some of the finest guns I had ever seen. Quite frankly I had not seen many but these were like a museum collection. And when I tell you that they knew everything about each gun I do mean everything.

We spent two hours or so just in front of the gun cabinets talking. I was receiving an education in firearms history. Who made them and in what country. The history of each gun and all the rest of it. It was at this time that Artie pulled out a large handgun. He said to me allow me introduce you to Harry. It was a 44 caliber that he had bought after seeing the movie Dirty Harry. Clint Eastwoods portrayal of Detective Harry Callahan's exploits.

This sucker was a hand cannon not a handgun. Artie said that in the morning we would shoot it. This was obviously his baby. And so in the morning after breakfast outside we went with Harry in hand. We must have shot a hundred rounds. My hands hurt. My shoulders hurt. And my ears were ringing. What a bitch that thing was.

We then walked over to one of the other buildings which we had not been in yesterday. As Artie swung the doors open there she was. A huge beast of a monster truck. Metal flake blue and glistening like a star. It had a cap of the same color and on both sides was sprayed the name Little Foot. How ironic this was to be as the story will unfold. It was his version of the original monster truck Big Foot. This was I believe a 69 Ford F250 powered by what he said was a blown 428 engine. It was in my opinion about 8 feet to the top of the cab and it was sitting on Dick Cepek 33 inch Mud Mothers. He had installed all kinds of blocks and shackles under the body. Everything and anything you could imagine to make the truck reach for the sky. I now realized that Artie had two babies named Harry and Little Foot. The exhaust system consisted of headers going into Cherry Bomb mufflers. And when he fired it up in the barn the timbers shook. The cab was accessed by billet aluminum steps and handrails. This truck was like an adult carnival ride. It was unbelievable! And for the duration of my stay Little Foot was to be our mode of transportation.

Artie took me everywhere. And I learned everything there was to know about the region. It had been a tremendous logging area. And up until just after World War II copper mining was a huge industry. He told me that the local mines produced more mineral wealth than the California gold rush had.

He also said that regionally speaking the forests were packed with black bears, wolves, moose, deer, gray and red foxes, bobcats, porcupines, hares, rabbits and everything else you can imagine. No wonder he told me to bring my shotgun. If my recollection is true it was also told to me that the French and Indian war had taken place here or in the surrounding area as well. We even took a boat ride to see Miners Castle and The Pictured Rocks which were gigantic and beautiful glacial formations.

Most of what we were seeing and doing was in an area called Munising. He brought me deep into areas of the woods. I don't remember if all of the forest was called Hiawatha or just a section of it. But it really doesn't matter. It was all the same being vast and dense. And not a soul could be seen anywhere. There were waterfalls both small and large located here and there. Artie said that something like 2 or 3% of the states total populace lived in this one area alone. Which represented a third of the state's total land mass. And because of this people were a sparse commodity here. And so it was that after two days of running around and having nothing short of a blast. We were back at the Raikonen homestead preparing for our camping, hiking and fishing adventure.

Out in the barn Artie took a small step ladder and placed it by the rear of Little Foot. He opened the tailgate and the cap. Inside of the bed he had already hooked us up. There was a fire extinguisher and a shovel. He had a first aid kit and a variety of ropes. One of the ropes he said was to hoist our perishable foods into a tree so the areas bears wouldn't get wind of them. He had two large water jugs. The kind you see at a little leaguers game. And there was a large cooler which we were going to fill with just ice. The rest was mainly canned items and some dry goods. As well as a case of Gatorade bottles and more than a few brews. On the interior sides of the bed Artie had built some racks made of wood. On one side there was a rack for long guns. And on the other side of the bed was a rack for fishing rods. He had already put in a pair of fly rods and several spinning rigs. I should also mention that he had electric winches on the front and rear of the truck. Hanging around here was like being in the fire department.

They had doubles of what they needed for everything. Talk about redundancy! And everything had its place. They were truly a remarkable family who were prepared for anything. And so having prepared ourselves with everything humanly imaginable we took off.

Artie said that we were heading to an area near Au Train Lake. The Au Train River being there as well. The way in was fairly long consisting of a decent dirt road which lead into some real four wheeler paths. And by the way did I mention the chainsaw in the truck? Which we had to break out on two occasions to clear some old downed timber from the trails. It was clear to me that nobody in a truck or any other kind of vehicle had been in here for a very long time. The trees we had cleared must have been laying where they were for years. The whole ordeal of getting in took us about two hours when finally we reached a small somewhat clear area for the camp. Now when I say clear it was more or less an opening in the standing pines. There was debris everywhere and the forest was a hodgepodge of pines both young and old. Artie said that many areas had been replanted. This being done after the logging industry had ravaged a fair amount of the forest.

We set up camp and dug a fire pit which really didn't take us much time at all. After which Artie said that there was still plenty of time left in the day for us to head down to the river and catch some trout. So we grabbed the fly rods. Artie took Harry and I grabbed my shotgun and we started walking and walking and walking. Just so you understand a long walk for me at this stage of my life in suburbia was going in and out of the mall. And maybe a two mile bike ride from time to time. I was shot. In any event we were getting close to our destination. Artie knew this because the forest started to tighten up. There were allot of smaller trees and bushes as we got closer to the water source. And there was no longer anything resembling a trail.

We were looking for breaks in the growth and fighting our way through the bramble when suddenly we broke out. Now we are not talking about the Colorado here. You could easily walk across the river. In fact as I looked up and down as far as I could. Many of the trees branches flanking the river's edge were not more that 8 or 10 feet from touching each other. This river or stream was strewn with wood and rocks. It was relatively calm flowing water and as I began to focus on the surface I could see that there were plenty of trout to be had. The two of us were using terrestrials which are flies that are tied to look like a variety of insects. You really couldn't cast much from anywhere in here. We were more or less flipping and mending the flies into position.

We must have been fishing for several hours. Both of us doing so very quietly enjoying the company of ourselves and the fish. It was really beautiful and I was more relaxed here and now than I had been in a very long time. It must have been about the time that I had fairly well zoned out of existence that I started to hear a loud rock clacking noise. To me it sounded as though it had to be very close.

I turned my head to look at Artie at the same time he had turned to look at me. He raised his hands in the... I don't know motion. We kept fishing and the sound kept happening. To me it sounded like two rocks cracking together against something being smashed. I could hear the crunch if you catch my drift? It reminded me of the breaking of a mussel shell as opposed to a clam. A mussels shell is much softer and thinner having a crunchier sound when broken. Slowly the two of us began walking towards each other. I was trying to look in the sounds direction but because of the tightness of the river with the overhanging branches and the rivers curvy nature. It made it impossible to see that far. Something or someone could have been 40 feet away and we would be unable to see them or it.

When we got close to each other we were basically lip synching. Artie thought it may have been moose antlers clacking together. And that the noise may well have been much further away than it sounded. So I slowly went back to the pool I was fishing in. This time positioning myself a little closer to the bank and my 12 gauge.

After a little while the noise had stopped. But now I could hear something moving about in the brush and it started to freak me out. I could see Artie craning his neck as well. We came together again and decided to wait a little bit and then split. Hoping that whatever was moving around would head on out of here while we waited and so we did. I was really on edge as we began fighting through this brush on the way out. I was expecting something to get the jump on us at any moment. And between holding the gear and shoving trees around there wouldn't be much time to mount and shoot if needed. It was at this time that I started to think of my old friend Dave. Fat

Dave I called him. I met him in a parking lot by a lake. I would go there to study in my car and would see Dave and some other guys who were always there. They were fishing with light tackle and worms catching bluegills and sun fish. Getting out of the car to stretch my legs and talk to them periodically I found out that he was from Florida. And with his tank top on I could see a large scar circumventing almost his entire shoulder. Now I happened to be studying for the medical field so I asked him what type of surgery he had.

He told me that while on tour in Vietnam he was on sentry duty. Walking back and forth on the camps perimeter. He and another G.I. would walk a half circle and meet again in the middle. Back and forth over and over again. As he was walking he heard a twig snap and as quickly as he turned some gook already had a bayonet buried in his shoulder. As he tried to move the Vietcong kept forcing the blade around in him. He was falling to the ground when instinctively with one arm he mustered up his M16 and emptied the entire clip into this creep killing him. And Dave was now lying on the ground with his shoulder hanging by a thread.

The rest is history as we say. Anyway I felt the same way right now. All the way back to the camp I had an eerie feeling and the forest was deathly quiet. You could barely here us walking let alone anything else. Finally we reached the camp and I began to make a fire while Artie stepped behind some trees to take care of business.

When he was through he was walking back and shouted in a somewhat startled fashion. What the Hell is that? As I walked over to see we stood there looking at a large snake on the ground which had a knot tied in its body on both ends. It looked like a snake dumbbell and it was still alive. There was absolutely no way these two knots were tied by the snake writhing around by itself. They were as tight as a rope knot. I don't remember now but I think that Artie said it was a blue snake of some sort. I would have to say taking into account the knots that it must have been six feet long. All that we could think of was who or what was in our camp while we were gone? It was mind boggling.

Artie took the snake and flung it into the woods. He said it would make a good meal for something. Now maybe it's because I am somewhat a city boy. But what concerned me did not seem to concern Artie at all. The clacking noises and now the snake. The feelings I was experiencing on the walk. And yet he was stone cold unmoving about any of it.

After spending a night around the campfire bullshitting about everything and anything under the sun. We stoked the fire one last time and crawled into the tent. I had my semi laying by my side and Artie had Harry next to his head.

It was sometime later in the night as Artie was cutting wood snoring. That I couldn't sleep a wink thinking about what had happened during the day. It was then that I started to hear some grunting or grumbling sounds outside the tent. It was hard to tell if they were near or far until a large shadow started to be cast between our tent and the fire. A shadow which after a few moments had completely darkened our tents interior. The darkening being followed by a large deep growl. And with this the top of the tent started to move downward. Artie had stopped snoring a moment earlier. I was fixed on the shadow and grabbed my gun. And before I could even think about it Artie sat up and squeezed of three successive rounds through the tent. The flash and concussion were unbelievable. And the smell of gunpowder and smoke filled the confines of the tent.

Whatever this was let out a scream which I can only describe as being that of a T. Rex. It was so loud that it shook me. The side of the tent was burning and the shadow was now gone as whatever this was sounded like it was running away. Screaming and bellowing as it did so into the distance. I remember unzipping the tent and bursting out with my gun. There was no way I was going to die without a fight in a tent. Artie leaped out behind me and the two of us stood there moving left and right looking and listening.

This beast was still screaming off in the distance. I was sure that Artie had nailed this sucker with three 44 caliber bullets at point blank range. If it was a black bear it would have dropped where it stood but it didn't. It ran away. I said to Artie what the hell could limp let alone run away with three 44 slugs in it? His answer was that bears can be tough mothers to take down. Now I had been thinking of doing exactly what he did. I was going to shoot also. But at that moment I had thought about it being some loser dude in the woods playing a really bad and possibly deadly prank.

We started looking around with flashlights for blood but we found nothing. And the ground was so hard that we couldn't see any prints. Not even those of our own boots. And beyond the glow of the fire the surroundings were as black as black could be. It was extremely unnerving to say the least. We got the fire going hot and heavy and stayed up the rest of the night. At this point I was ready to call it quits. But I didn't want Artie to think I had no balls. Besides all of that I was the city slicker. We were supposed to have nuts of steel. Right? We had three days left according to our game plan. So in the morning after sunrise. Artie having brushed off everything that happened during the night. Said to me let's head over by the lake today. And so we grabbed our spinning rods and our guns of course. And headed off to the closest side of the lake. This time his direction took us through a marginally more open tract of woods until we got nearer to the lake. Then the undergrowth thickened up like it had by the river.

At any rate we positioned ourselves along the lakes edge and started to throw some poppers and spinners and got into some fairly decent action. The sun was out on the lake and it was nice to be out from under the canopy of the pines. But while we were fishing I was noticing from time to time, in particular over the first two hours that we were there. Something large and dark in color peering in and out of the bushes along the far side of the lake. First in one place and then in another.

I kept pointing in its direction as I would see it. And saying to Artie do you see that? And then again. Hey look over there! And for all of my prompting he saw nothing. But I definitely saw something that was alive and moving. And I couldn't get my mind off the campsite incident last night. We must have fished for about 6 hours or so taking a few food and drink breaks in between. When Artie said that we should head back. And maybe we could do a little varmint hunting before the sunset. It sounded like a good idea so we began the long walk back.

By the time we had gotten back to the vicinity of the camp we had been gone about 8 or 9 hours. And I might add we had heard and seen nothing out of the ordinary other than whatever I was looking at by the lake. As the camp came into view ahead of us I couldn't believe what I was looking at. The entire campsite including the truck had been ransacked. Everything was thrown about. There were things thrown up in the trees and our cooler was completely flattened on the ground. It looked as though a steam roller ran over it. The truck was cosmetically in ruins. The cap looked like a tree fell on it and both of the side windows were blown out. The truck's cab had been smashed down so severely that we could not open the driver's door.

And there was no evidence of a log or anything that would have or could have been used to do the damage. The tailgate was folded down and under the rear bumper. And one side of the gate was torn from the body having the hinge still attached to it. The front winch was torn completely from the bumper. I am talking about 9/16 bolts and washers being ripped cleanly out of the steel bumper. And the other winch had all of the cable pulled out of it. This cable was not just yanked out but it was completely detached from the housing. Both of the aluminum steps were torn off and we were only able to find one of them in a mangled state. But thank God the cab had not been opened. The front of the hood from the grill inward looked as though it was hit with three or four blows from a 12 inch wide tree trunk. I say this because I have no other way to describe what we were looking at.

And having said as much there was not a single indicator such as bark, chips or even any marks on the vehicle. Which would have indicated that part of a tree was actually used to wreak the destruction. There were no small dents whatsoever. Just large, long and wide blows to the metal work. What bothered me most of all was the type of power that would be needed to flatten a large Igloo cooler. It looked like it was compressed in a trash compactor. And the fact that large bolts had been torn away from the truck leaving a reverse dimple where they had been in the steel was insane. Whatever did this was not an individual or a group of individuals. No man could have done this. There was nothing to say we were simply aghast.

There was now nothing we could do with all of the debris. The cap was caved in and the tailgate was destroyed. I jumped up into the bed and tried to push up on the broken cap in an effort to open the bed back up a bit. I was forcing my back against the broken roof of the cap. And as I worked my way into position I noticed something very odd. Caught in the very end of one of the cracks in the fiberglass were several very long dark colored hairs. As though something with hair had lost a few while their body slid or dragged off of the roof. I showed them to Artie and he said to me that isn't black bear fur. Its way too long. These strands were like 8 or 10 inches in length. He just shook his head and I understood.

We were shell shocked and his beautiful truck was trashed. We gathered up all of the stuff we could and shoved it up under the remnants of the cap into the bed. We grabbed the tailgate and flexed it back and forth until we could twist it up and into the bed. When we came into camp everything was neatly organized. And as we were about to leave it looked like an open trash can.

Artie had climbed up into the cab from the passenger's side which was not an easy task without the step. He started brushing the shattered glass off the seat and everywhere else. The truck started right up and he let it run. I guess about an hour had gone by since we came back to the camp and it was time to get the heck out of here. It was a long ride in and it would be a longer ride out. As we left I couldn't help feeling really bad for Artie in a number of ways. After all I came on his invitation. And now his truck was in ruins and we were leaving with our tails between our legs. What would his family think? What would anyone think?

When we finally got clear of the woods we started heading down the road when at some point we saw a cop coming the other way and Artie waved him down. As he stopped I couldn't see him because of the trucks height. He being on Arties side and down in his car. But I heard him say what the hell happened to you guys? Artie shut the truck down as I jumped out and he followed. We spent about 45 minutes walking around the truck and telling the officer our tale. He wrote up an incident report and gave us a copy. He said to us that there is shit in these woods that we know nothing about.

Later on as we entered his property as you would well imagine everyone came out to see the truck and talk to us about our ordeal. It was at dinner that evening when his father began telling us about what his father had said to him. He told us that the loggers and miners had spun many a yarn about giant hairy creatures. Creatures that they saw in the timber. He said his father told him that they would mess with and damage their equipment. Typically doing so when they had left for the day. They would come back and find machinery bent and broken. And he said that this was a regular happening for the workers. He said that the men would speak of things being thrown into the camp without being able to see who or what threw them.

At any rate that's my story. Artie and I still speak to this day and he actually rebuilt his baby...Little Foot. Arties father took the hairs that we retrieved and framed them in their den for family posterity. I have never been back to visit Artie since.

The Shenandoah Park Sighting

As I begin this segment I thought I would mention beforehand. So that you the reader do not think that I the writer have some type of Clint Eastwood fetish. It is purely a coincidence that this next witness and the prior witness had both mentioned the name of the actor. I think it's just a testimonial of how great an impact that these spaghetti westerns had on many of us societally especially the men. And without any further ado I introduce you to Robert Woods. As he begins to tell us of his encounter.

I guess as I begin I should tell you how it was that I came to be where I was when I saw the beast in Shenandoah Park. My wife had divorced me some time before. And rather than sitting around and moping about the whole grizzly affair. And I do mean grizzly. I took up exercising. Some weight lifting and bike riding to be more precise. As well as allot of walking. After about a year or so I was clocking about 5 or 6 miles a day just in walking alone. And I was actually quite fast if I do say so myself. The speed actually developed out of necessity because I had limited time to take my walks due to my work schedule and everything else that was going on in my life at that time. It was because I was so committed to not slacking off about how far I was walking. That I increased my speed to ensure that the same amount of miles would be attained every time out. The fact of the matter being this. That over a period of about 3 years I was fitter than I had ever been in my entire life. So something good had come to life out of what was a hideous divorce. Well as it turns out my next phase was to begin to push the limits of what I could do. And I decided that when I could get time off I would take little 4 or 5 day vacations going to areas where I could actually hike and see something. For up to this point in time the only thing I was seeing was the surrounding homes in my community.

And so my trip to Shenandoah was actually one of many hiking destinations I had been on. It began as most did by contacting the park and sending for a brochure. After which I would scope out what type of accommodations were available. The preferred being camping in or near the location of the hike. And then I would plan my trip accordingly. Having gone through my punch list my plan for Shenandoah was this. I was going to set up camp at a place called Big Meadows. From there I would walk the area between it and Thornton Gap. I would be walking on a section of the Alleghany Trail where there seemed to be some fairly good elevation. Up to about 4000 ft. according to the map. The route that I had chosen was spotted with many overlooks as well as some interesting things to see along the hike and to me it looked perfect. Just enough of a challenge for where I was physically at the time. What a beautiful place this seemed to be in the brochure. It was late summer and my hope was that there wouldn't be too many people there hiking while I was. I thought this because the brochure touted some staggering visitor numbers annually. And in my heart I had always envisioned myself living the life of the guy in High Plains Drifter. Confident and alone. Able to handle whatever came my way. Well this was as close to that as I would get. I was the High Trails Drifter one day at a time. And this was to be my first days hike in Shenandoah.

My goal was to make it to a place called Corbin Cabin after which I would trek back to camp. The scenery was breathtaking as I made my way to the cabins location. To get there you had to cross a street and a small creek breaking of from the Alleghany Trail. The cabin itself was located near the base of Pinnacle Peak in a place called Nicolson's Hollow. When I had finally arrived at the cabin I was amazed at how much guts it must have taken for someone to not only come here. But to build this miniature homestead by hand so many years ago. It was a small cabin built on a stone foundation of sorts. It had one main room with a small side addition. There was a fire place and a porch and each one of the cabins timbers was hand hewn. I could only imagine the amount of labor involved in constructing it and the brochure said it had been inhabited by an old mountaineer.

Now that dude was more like the High Plains Drifter. Having met my goal or half way point I started to head back. It had been a great day and by the time I made it back to the campsite I was bushed. The next day I packed up and drove north a short distance to the Thornton Gap entrance station. This time I was going to hike from the other direction. From the north down towards Corbin Cabin again and back. In this way I would have covered a fairly nice section of the trail in two day hikes. And so once again I took off for the day's journey. There was a considerable amount of wildlife that was visible along the route. I had brought with me my Nikon 20 x 50 binoculars. They are a bit bulky but well worth the effort and extra weight. I was encountering many deer off the side of the trail here and there. And the birds here for the most part were very different from those seen where I live as can be expected when one travels to different regions of the states. I was so glad that I came here. I had just passed the area where yesterday I had cut off for Corbin Cabin and I pushed on a little further until I reached a spot called Stony Man. The elevation here was about 4000 ft. and I sat down for a rest.

The vistas from here were incredible. Rolling hills and woods as far as the eyes could see. The sun was bright and I felt more alive than I had ever been. I was eating some granola bars and drinking water when I decided to break out the Nikons and have a look see. At one point I had put them down and was just looking with my eyes when I noticed two black objects in a clearing way off in the distance below. It was then that I realized they were both moving.

So I picked up the binoculars and focused in on them. I would have to say they were about a 1000 yards away from where I was perched and I was watching them for quite a while. It was a large black bear and a cub and they were feasting on what appeared to be a deer carcass. Now of course I hadn't seen the bear take the deer down and I was wondering if the deer had just died and they sniffed it out for a meal. I must have been watching them for 15 or 20 minutes. Now I must warn you that the next series of events happened so quickly that it was actually quite difficult to figure out just what happened. Within the binoculars field of view while my eyes were transfixed on the bears. A large and darkly colored figure came running into the frame.

And I do mean running. I don't know how much ground it actually covered but it looked like perhaps 75 yards in 2 or 3 seconds. Not only was this thing was booking but it was running on two legs. At the same time the figure was running into my field of view I saw the larger bear lurch and jump to the side of the carcass as the little one bolted away. This all happened in matter of seconds.

The creature closed the gap between itself and the bear quickly and ended the sprint making head on contact with the bear knocking it to the ground. It was now on top of the bear and I saw what appeared to be its arms moving rather quickly in a flailing type of motion. It looked like some blows were being thrown by the darkly colored creature and then everything stopped. It was now sitting still on top of the bear straddling its body. A minute later the cub reappeared at a distance. And I saw the creature lifting and waving its arms. From the distance that I was away not a sound could be heard. I simply saw the cub standing in one place and the creature lifting its arms up and waving them. Moments later the cub scurried into the brush and was out of sight for good. I continued to watch for about 30 minutes. The creature that was still sitting on the bear was now tossing the bears head back and forth in its two hands. Now I don't know how tall a bear is from the ground to the top of its back.

But I would have to say that in the brief time I saw the creature running into view. That it was at least 3 times as tall as the bear was high. So if the bear was 3 feet tall this creature was 9 or 10 feet tall. It was immense. Its arm hang almost looked to be as long as the bear's total body length. I knew I was now looking at with my own eyes a Bigfoot. A Bigfoot that had just charged and killed a black bear. I watched the creature for about another 15 minutes but time was not on my side. As awesome as this was I was going to have to leave at some point having to complete my return hike back before it got dark. A task which I was already wondering if I could complete.

I snapped a few photos with my Canon camera. But I must admit that I didn't have any great hopes for the development of the pictures. Never the less I took a few hoping for the best. The Bigfoot stayed sitting on the bear the entire time. It was very weird and very surreal. Eventually I got up and left knowing that I would really have to step up the pace on the return leg to make it back by dark. And thankfully I was up to the task. When I made it back to Thornton Gap I stopped by the ranger station. I had actually tipped in there to say hello before I began my hike and had told them my plans for the day. You always want to let others know where you are and what you plan to do. God forbid something should happen on the way. I told the rangers what had transpired and they were dumfounded. One of them told me that he had seen something a few years ago. But he stopped talking before elaborating on just what exactly that something was. At this time I asked Rob to elaborate as much as possible. On any details about the Bigfoot he could recollect. And here is what he said. As I mentioned before this thing covered a large amount of real estate rapidly. Now I know I am just throwing numbers at you. Numbers which I have no way of actually knowing or calculating. But it looked like it was running 40 mph across this tract of land. It also looked like the bear was taken completely by surprise which also indicated to me a very fast run.

All that the bear had time to do was shift off of the carcass and turn. And then it was hit and hit hard. The impact reminded me of Ronny Lott plugging a run on the football field. I mean it was WHAMO! And lights out. And just think about it for a moment.

The thought of any man being there and performing such an act is utterly ludicrous. This creature did not hesitate for one split second. He didn't run up to the bear stopping to size up his attack. It was a brutally effective running kill.

The other thing was this. I could clearly see the entire time the borders if you will of exactly who was who. The Bigfoot was a reddish dark brown and the bear was black so there was no difficulty at all in telling the positions of the two beasts. In other words who was moving and who was not. I wish I could have stayed to see which carcass the Bigfoot would drag off if not both. But I was out of time as you can understand. By the way when I had arrived back home I had developed the film. At the same time I had a couple of the prints enlarged. Unfortunately as I suspected it was a wasted effort. Even when enlarged you could only see a small dark spot where the two creatures were. But for me that was good enough for memories sake. Because I knew what the small dark spot represented. And so my readers what an awesome sighting.

And I might add also proof positive of what I stated in the beginning. He saw what he saw because he took the time to stop and look. If he had kept hiking watching only the path with the surrounding trees, deer and birds. He would have missed this event entirely.

✗

The Fitzpatrick Wilderness Sighting

The following is the account of events which was given to me by Allister and Marjorie Macnab. Allister was a transplant from Scotland who was hired for his scientific abilities by a firm in New Hampshire. It was during his employment that he met up with and married his wife to be Marjorie Tennyson. Who also happened to have a smidgeon of Scottish in her ancestry. It is actually Allister's passion for fly fishing which he had imported from Scotland that brings us to our stories beginning in the state of Wyoming. In an area known as the Fitzpatrick Wilderness adjacent with the Shoshone National Forest. From this point forward it is the Macnabs who will be telling their story in their own way. I will not bother to differentiate between who is talking and when.

My wife and I had been in Wyoming three times in the past. This was to be our fourth fly fishing adventure in the region. Wyoming contains quite simply some of the best fly fishing and wilderness hiking in the world and it is frankly breathtaking country. We quickly had learned after our first trip that it is well worth your time and money to work with a good outfitter or guide service. When you are planning to go into such areas the fact of the matter is this. In most if not all situations you will need some type of permits and or licenses. And regardless of where or when you go you will also need some firearms and gear. Additionally the area knowledge of local men or women is a valuable asset which cannot be measured in dollars and cents. This is not the time or place to be cheap. For the price of a Hawaiian vacation for two you can be readily supplied with everything and anything that you will need including a guide. And in doing so you are not only helping yourselves. But you are supporting an industry and a people in the region which will ensure that going into the future these resources will be in place for a very long time.

We met up with our guide Joseph at a predetermined location. He was a slightly built rugged looking man who was of pure Arapaho heritage. His family had been in this region for many generations and although he looked Indian he spoke like any other American. We were to hike into and fish in two different areas. The first sight that we would fish was named Big Meadows and the second along the route would be Downs Fork Meadows. There is a creek running right through this area which changes its name periodically as you trek. The only name I can ever remember is Dinwoody Creek simply because of the name and its European roots. Each time we come to this state we prospect a new area so this location was brand new for the two of us. The area consists of a rocky mountainous surround with pine forests, grassy meadows and water. That's Wyoming and that's why we love it. We each were given a holstered pistol and Joseph had a rifle and a pistol as well. This is grizzly country and there are plenty of visible herd animals and trout as well. Creatures which the bears are itching to sink their claws into. So its eyes wide open from here on out.

The entire area that we would pass through is virtually the same in appearance throughout. Thick grassy meadows and or marshy areas. Surrounded and or flanked by some extremely rugged timber. Beyond which rocky mountainous terrain rises up behind the trees. The lands appearance was this way in every direction that you looked and walked. This trip was in no way particularly difficult. The actual mileage covered was not at all that far. It was more a casual type of hike with most of the time being focused on catching trout. We hiked in and set up camp on the edge of Big Meadows. From where we were in the timberline we had a good firm patch of ground on which to pitch a tent. Which would be within a reasonable walking distance across the meadow for us to reach the creek. Right behind the stretch of forest where we had set up our camp was what I will call a small mountain jutting up from the earth. And across from the creek in front of us there was a lake that you could see off to the right. During the first two days we had spotted a grizzly coming down across the meadow. It was posing no threat to us and was fairly far away each time that we saw it. We also saw a moose grazing on the thick green grass. I had told Allister on more than one occasion that having a guide brought a certain sense of stability to us whenever we saw something. In particular the bear because the guide provided us with an air of calmness. Joseph was not by any means flustered by what may have frightened us to death.

He simply had a mutual respect for the surroundings and its inhabitants. Which is not to say that Joseph was foolhardy or lax in any way. He simply was not visibly moved. On one afternoon we were lined up side by side fishing the bank of the creek. All of us were facing in the direction of this small lake which I believe was northwest. Next to the lake there was an outcropping of rock which butted up against it. Let's call it a rugged looking hill or mound. Perhaps it was 200 feet tall at best which was much smaller than the surrounding mountainous landscape. Marjorie and I were standing with our eyes focused into the creek when suddenly Joseph said… Look over there! Right by the edge of that hill. Do you see it? We both stopped and looked trying to follow the direction of Josephs point. Then he said it again. Do you see it? It's a Hairy man. Now Marjorie and I were not ignorant of what he was talking about or pointing at. Although neither of us had seen one we knew he was talking about a Bigfoot. And as we focused in on the base of the mound there it was loping along the edge of the hill adjacent to the marsh. It was very easy to observe once we laid eyes on it for it was completely out in the open. It must have come out of the woods a short distance to the north of our camp.

And it had more than likely walked right across the meadow while we were fishing. We hadn't seen it and yet there it was. I would say that it was 5 or 6 hundred yards away and the outline of the creature was unmistakable. The marsh or meadow area consisted of bright green grass that was about 2 feet tall. Grass that was especially green along the water's edge which abutted the rocky outcropping. There were no trees or anything else to obscure our view and the Bigfoots profile was very dark against the rocky background. The rocks being beige and light brown in color. Its arms were swinging like a clocks pendulum. It was taking long and deliberate strides in combination with arm swings to match them. It also was walking with a somewhat forward leaning posture which was quite evident to the eye.

Within two minutes it was gone from our view around a bend and we had just become members of the club. The rest of the day and evening was spent with the three of us talking about Bigfoot. And pardon the pun but this was a really BIG deal for me and my wife. That night around the campfire Joseph started telling us of Indian folklore and such pertaining to these hairy men. He had actually seen them many times himself. But that's not to say he was not as surprised as we were to see it. But it was more matter of fact for him then it was for us. This was an absolutely incredible experience. Joseph had added during the night that we would have to keep our eyes out for the Hairy man now while we were here. He said that the Indian people had experienced and spoke of some really bad things regarding these creatures in their history. For their tribal records had recorded many encounters including attacks on people, livestock and even disappearances of people being attributed to them.

We could hear it in the tone of his voice and we were now certain that he really was not too happy that this sighting had occurred. I also took note that he spent a fair amount of time that evening cleaning and prepping the guns for action. The next day we packed up and basically walked to the back of the lake where the Bigfoot had disappeared from view. Joseph said that over there we would pick up on Glacier Trail. Otherwise we would have been trekking entirely through the woods to get to the next location. I wouldn't have known one way or the other. This is just another reason why we pay the professionals like Joseph to guide us. From there we would make our way north to an area called Downs Fork Meadows. Now I would be a liar if I didn't say to you that when we started down this route things became a whole lot creepier. Not just because of what we had seen but this trail area suddenly became quite a bit tighter.

Everything had kind of closed in on us.

There were large stands of timber flanking us on both sides as well as some rock walls cropping up here and there forming what felt like a prison cell around us. It was a kind of curvy trail as I remember and it was difficult to see that far ahead of us at any given point. The thought kept running through my mind of the old westerns where the Indians would set up an ambush point on the unsuspecting cowboy's. Positioning themselves behind some boulders up on a cliff. Sorry Joseph! Dinwoody Creek was now just ahead of us in the timber off to our right. And to get there we went straight into a somewhat dark stand of trees for a short time. We then found ourselves winding around some more ambush points or high rocks and as we came out of the trees we were near a fork in two creeks. The Downs Fork Creek and the south end of Honeymoon Creek or very close to it. I just remember Joseph saying something about Honeymoon Creek and us joking around about it. This was really quite a cool little area. There were several meadows with a number of creeks or streams meandering around within them. They were like small tributaries off the main creeks and the meadows had several stands of trees here and there within them as well. It was like something out of a fairy tale.

I know I speak for all of us when I say that this place really struck us all in the most amazing way. It was kind of like Alice going down the rabbit hole and popping out in a wonderland. And I remember kidding Joseph about what the difference was between a creek and a stream? Now just so you understand Joseph's job was not to fish. In fact numerous times we had asked him to join us with a rod and he just said no thank you. He would spot for us or get in the creek and help with landing a fish. And he paid strict attention to other things like setting up our flies and leaders. But in Downs Fork he was seemingly preoccupied with his field glasses. When I asked him about this preoccupation he said that this was real grizzly territory and that it would be best for all if he kept watch. Who were we to argue? It was during the latter part of the afternoon when something let out the loudest most prolonged howling roar that is humanly imaginable. It was like living near the fire department when the siren goes off. The howl was as intense as you could possibly imagine and it sounded really close. Now there was quite a bit more of thick forest here going in all directions. And the truth be told the sound seemed like it was emanating from all around us rather than in any particular direction.

It was the loudest most enveloping blast of noise that I had ever heard in my life and it brought us to a complete standstill. Yes it's all true. Allister and I stood there completely aghast. All of us had our jaws open and Joseph had already brought his rifle to bear. We dropped our rods and grabbed our pistols. I was trembling and then it was dead silence. I mean we heard nothing. We simply stood looking and turning in every direction while not saying a word. It seemed like 15 minutes had passed when Joseph finally broke the silence.

He turned towards us and whispered… The hairy man is here. I remember thinking to myself that even when holding a gun one can sometimes feel defenseless. And that is exactly how I felt at that moment in time. As far as I was concerned whatever had made that noise could eat bullets and spit them back out again. We had a momentary discussion about our desire to not stay there any longer and we started back out the way we came in through the trees, ambush points and everything else. Only this time we were like jungle fighters with guns drawn. We high tailed it all the way back and through Big Meadows and believe me when I tell you we were speed hiking.

Nobody said anything thing about needing to drink or eat. It was all about moving and moving fast. I guess it must have been about 2 miles south of Big Meadows when we broke out into an area that was not that secluded. What I mean to say is that we could virtually see in every direction and fairly well. And so knowing we would have to spend the night like it or not this was the place to set camp. When I tell you we had an uneasy night that is an understatement. Nobody would or could sleep and Joseph felt it was his duty regardless of what we did to be awake and standing guard. That night the minutes seemed like hours. I kept waiting for a Banzai attack and nothing happened. In the morning we did actually take time to eat because we were all hungry and would need all of our energy in order to finish the final stretch out doing so as quickly as possible. To this very day we still send Joseph a Christmas card to let him know we are thinking about him. And as for my wife and I we have not been back to Wyoming in over 15 years.

And we won't be going there any time soon either. The Macnabs told me at the end of my interview that they will only fish in more open and somewhat rural locations now. And typically within the confines of a town or near a highway or the like. At the end I asked them what aspect stood out the most about this encounter and here was Marjorie's response. Nothing imaginable to the human mind or spirit could prepare you or help you when the screaming started. It almost felt like it was coming down from the sky on top of us. The scream to me felt like it would hurt me. It was like some sort of sound weapon. I know this doesn't make any sense to you but if a child was there I think they would have just balled up on the ground and started crying. It was absolutely terrifying and certainly something that we will never ever forget. The two of us talk regularly about Joseph having to go back into these areas again and again. It's how he makes a living and he is one brave hombre.

✕

The Rock Hounds Encounter

Many of you may already be saying to yourselves. What on earth is a rock hound? Well a rock hound is an individual who enjoys hunting and scavenging for rocks, gems, fossils, semi-precious stones and or minerals around the globe. And this story is about the Saladinos. Anthony and Debbie to be more precise. I actually drove to their home in order to do this interview. And I must say that they had amassed quite the collection of the aforementioned in their travels around the states. From here on out this is their story as it was told to me by the couple face to face.

We had planned around the month of May well over 20 years ago. To head down to Aurora North Carolina for the Megalodon shark tooth dig. In case you are unfamiliar with the name the Megalodon was the largest pre-historic shark on record. With sizes ranging up to 60 feet in length. And nice quality unbroken fossil teeth from this behemoth are considered prize possessions by enthusiasts. Now you can purchase them from those who have already done the hunting. The prices actually being quite reasonable. But as is generally the case in all things collectable the fun is in the hunting. So we packed the truck and headed down to the event. We were going to spend two weekdays there and head back home. We chose during the week because the weekends are usually jammed with people. Now it's not much of a hunt there but you still have to do allot of work. There is a place there called the PCS phosphate mine and what they do is this. They bring out tons of fossil laden dirt.

And the people who come are allowed to sift through the spoils in the hope of finding an intact Megalodon tooth. Teeth which are in fact found all of the time by people at this event. Most of the teeth however are broken in pieces. And the whole ones which are found are generally between ½ to 4 inches in length. Overall it's kind of a neat community type of affair. You can meet and talk to allot of like-minded hounds from all over the nation and in fact the world. Many of the people who were present had traveled there as had we. While we were there my husband and I had gotten to know a couple by the name of Tyler from Oregon. They asked us if we had ever been to their home state and we told them that we had not. Although we had heard there may be some very good pickings there.

This fact they confirmed to us. So we exchanged numbers and addresses with them and they told us that if we ever find ourselves up in their neck of the woods. That we should feel free to look them up or at the very least call them and ask for some good locations in the state to scrounge around in. Our own collection which we showed to Bill during this interview consists of about 70 or 80 pieces. About 40 or so were our own finds and the rest were pieces which we have purchased throughout the years. The Tyler's on the other hand boasted a collection of over a thousand pieces most of which were found in Oregon. I didn't have to ask my husband if we would place Oregon on our destinations list we just looked at each other and knew that we would. It was two years later that we contacted the Tyler's and planned to head out there for a week. Now here are some helpful guidelines which we have been putting into practice for many years. They came from a wonderfully created guide for the hunt. These are the rules for safe and effectual rock hounding.

Firstly it is always advisable to select several sites within a fairly small area. This will help you in not wasting too much of your valuable time travelling from place to place. In addition it is always wise to become as informed as possible on what exactly can potentially be found in each location that you plan to search in.

Secondly you should not hesitate to inquire of other local collectors or clubs in the area. They can be a vast resource of information for your own personal hunt and most are more than willing to share what they know with fellow hounds.

Thirdly you must bring proper tools and or equipment including boots and tough clothing for field work. And depending on what type of material you are seeking you may need a rock hammer, shovel, pry bar, sledge hammer and chisel. Or perhaps even a light pick mattock. If you plan to pan for gold panning supplies of course will be necessary as well. We also like to have a small sieve. Which is generally nothing more than some screening attached over a 2x4 frame. Fourthly you must make preparations for seasonable and unseasonable weather conditions. Canteens, caps and sunglasses for hotter more arid areas and warmer gear for mountainous and colder climates. And of course rain gear. Also check out where you are going as far as who the land belongs to. You may have to get permission from local landowners to be there. Take care in and around abandoned mines. Don't throw any rocks or debris from cliffs or hillsides. And take only what you will use leaving the rest behind for others. These are the rules we abide by and if you do the same you will have good success and be safe in doing so.

My husband and I had decided to set our sights on an area surrounding the Clackamas River located near Estacada Oregon. The river also had near it a moderate hiking trail that was about 10 miles in and out. This area was well known by our friends the Tyler's to contain cinnabar, petrified wood and jaspers. And the river is also frequented by whitewater kayakers and hikers alike. We made our way into the surrounding area with our camper.

We have an older Dodge with what I would call a half camper in the bed. It's not self-contained but it's a place to crash after a day of hunting. We have a Coleman gas stove and a porta potty inside. As well as a small propane heater that keeps it quite toasty when needed. Generally we look for places where we can park without much of a hassle and in rural areas it's actually quite easy. On this trip we really got lucky. We nestled in at a campground called Indian Henry which is just past Pup Fall. From there we could easily access what's called the Riverside Trail. A trail which was about 6 miles in and out. A bit shorter of a hike than our previously planned location. The Riverside Trail twists and turns alongside the Clackamas River and at times it comes right down to it crossing it as well. We decided on the first day to do an exploratory hike. This was done so that we could see if there were any noticeable hot spots. Doing a preliminary hike enables us to focus our time and energy wisely once we have determined the best areas to search.

This place was beautiful. At times you could hear road traffic but as the trail meandered around through the forest the sounds of cars would fade away. There were areas that were high above the river from which you could hear rushing water below you. This was an old growth forest and you couldn't see much ahead of you or off to the sides. Your vision being obscured by the large pines and undergrowth which were everywhere. And the way the path undulated around it seemed like most of the time you were going up a little grade and then coming back down. Over and over again the trail was winding like a serpent through the forest. As it turns out we were not alone in there this day. Which is not to say that it was a mob scene by any means. But I would say that we ran into a few dozen people during the days hike. At days end having done our due diligence on our reconnaissance run. We had located several prime areas for exploration. We also had scoped out some viable river bars which we felt would be accessible with hip waders.

The forest in most places was hard up against the river's edge with the exception of few locations where there were rounded rocks and small boulders visible like the sand on a seashore. Rocks which formed somewhat of a bank on the edges of the river. These bars and bank areas are prime locations for good pickings in our trade. The river carries everything down stream and the rocky and bar areas are collection or catch points for anything and everything coming down river. Places where things have generally gotten hung up and buried through the years. This entire area was what my husband and I referred to as The Land of the Lost. Naming it after the old Hollywood movie where if you let your imagination run wild you could picture a Stegosaurus or a Sabre Tooth Tiger sneaking around in the undergrowth. Gigantic wide trees were everywhere.

And clusters of broad leaf ferns were here and there wherever you would walk. Decaying fallen trees and limbs were strewn about the forest floor in every direction. This was truly a very neat little piece of paradise.

The next day we headed down to an area by the river that had looked promising the day before. And I feel as though I must add this as well. Do you know the feeling you have when someone is watching you? I think we all do. Well we feel this all the time when we are hounding. And generally when we look up there are a couple of people somewhere watching us at work. Whenever people see us we are like celebrities. Everyone one wants to watch us doing what we do. And they all want to know what we are looking for and how we find them. This is just part of the wonderful social aspect involved in the hunt. It was actually getting late and the truth be told we hadn't found much of anything worth keeping. The reality being that this is generally the case in the life of a rock hound. It's not as though there are valuable pieces of this and that waiting for you to put them in your bag everywhere you go. And under every stone that you flip over. If that was the case we would be multimillionaires not rock hounds. But perseverance does pay off occasionally. For near the days end my wife said to me. Oh my goodness! Look at this honey. She had just found a magnificent piece of dark green bloodstone. A stone which is generally associated with the common opal. It was a fantastic find. A find which may very well be the best piece in our collection to date.

This was a grand slam in rock hunting and we were grinning from ear to ear as we hugged each other. And so it was that we left the river for the day and hiked back to our camper. It was a great end to a great day. And if our trip had ended right here and now we would have been more than happy having found this beautiful bloodstone but it didn't. The next day we were to stumble upon our greatest discovery ever and it wasn't a rock or a fossil. The following day there was a dreary and drizzly rain to contend with. The two of us however are not easily deterred from our hunts so we donned our raingear and headed on out. This day was very different as we headed down the trail. There was not a soul around as we commenced our hike.

We had the entire place to ourselves. It was awesome and at the same time a little bit eerie to be in there alone. When we arrived at this days prospecting site we had been digging about for some three hours or so when we heard an air horn blast. This meant that someone else was actually walking about in the area. And they had either seen a bear or something else that they wanted to scare off with the blast of this horn. Many people including ourselves carry a small boat horn when hiking. One loud blast will generally send anything scurrying for cover. But the horn blast was an eye opener for us. An eye opener in that number one we were not alone. And number two being that a bear was potentially around. When we are in the zone as hounds. Very little is said between us with the exception of the occasional have you seen anything? It's somewhat of an out of body experience. You are totally at peace and one with the work. And there is always this sense of expectancy as though you are reading a lottery ticket hoping that the next line will contain the winning numbers.

If my memory serves me well I think that we both stood up and turned at the same time. I heard what sounded like a deep ugggh sound accompanied by a splash. And as we now stood looking. About maybe 75 feet away from us standing in the river's edge was a Sasquatch. It turned immediately to look at us. I truly don't believe it knew we were there. I believe it had just stepped into the river from the brush. And up until that point in time we had heard and seen nothing except the horn blast. The Sasquatch seemed to be as shocked to see us as we were to see it. My husband and I were frozen in fear. The creature wasn't moving at first. It was just staring at us. And then it started slowly swaying or rocking back and forth from the waist. It made a couple of guttural sounds that were deep and my husband crept over to my side. Now you will just have to take my word for it. For if you ever find yourself in this situation you simply do not know what to do. We were totally vulnerable and as I just said frozen with fear. This thing was easily well over 10 feet tall. I remember that I had actually closed my eyes once or twice. I kept hoping I would wake up or something. I was thinking that this was somehow not happening. How could it be happening? But it was and we were now in the middle of it.

Its face looked very mean and intimidating. It had black deeply inset eyes. Eyes that were the size of golf balls. Anthony you tell him the rest. You're better at this than I am. Well it's difficult to put into words everything that you see and experience at a time like this. It's surreal and extremely frightening to find yourself in such a situation. And part of you is continually saying that this can't be happening and yet it is. The shear immensity of this beast was staggering. It was like standing alongside of a Clydesdale horse.

I mean the bulk and dimensions of the creature were at the extremes of human cognizance. It had to have been nearing 5 feet wide at the shoulders and the waist area was 3 to 4 feet in width. Am I right honey? Yes you are. I would have to throw the numbers of 1500 to 2000 lbs. as being its weight at you. I would say that's its arms alone were 6 feet long. And the hands on this thing were as large as a hockey goalies glove. Absolutely massive in every sense of the word. Its head was about 16 inches wide and it tapered slightly up to the top. The head was also set deeply into the shoulders. There was no visible neck like a human. The shoulder muscles were enormous. It looked like a large loaf of bread was sitting on either side of its head. That was how big its muscles were. I mean everything about it was beyond human comprehension. There is nothing that can prepare you for this type of thing. The entire event was completely overpowering to the senses.

What skin that was visible was somewhat gray and it was mostly covered with longer darker brown to black splotches of hair. We could see everything about it and clearly because of it being so close. And there are no ifs ands or buts about what we are saying. This was and is the real deal my friend. Up close and personal. It was after what seemed like an eternity that a second creature came protruding out of the brush.

The upper part of its body and arms were all we could see. It did not step into the river but rather stood in place watching us. This one was about one to two feet smaller than the one in the river. But also every bit as massive in its own rite. And when this second one appeared there was a strong stench of feces in the air which was not the case with the first. The upper arms of both of these beasts looked like an average boy's waistline. One being bigger than the other. And then suddenly the one in the river kind of flexed its upper body like a strong man's pose while letting out a large deep huff and a grunt. While both arms moved forward with its fists clenched.

And then without warning. As suddenly as all of this had begun. It turned and took one step into the brush while at the same moment the other one withdrew and it was all over. We heard nothing more. I mean not so much as a whisper. They had vanished like two ghosts. We couldn't even hear them departing. But then again we hadn't heard them arriving either. We stood wondering for about 30 minutes. Wondering where they were and if they were possibly alongside of us watching our every move. I whispered to my wife maybe whoever had blown the horn had seen them or part of them passing through the woods and thought they were seeing a bear. We slowly gathered together our gear and made our way out. One of the craziest aspects of this in our minds was where and how everything had happened. The two of us had been in many much more desolate and lonely locations.

What I mean to say is this. Yes this was a large and old forest. I told you it felt like a dinosaur could be roaming around. But outside of the confines of the park and the trail there were some roads and many fairly open tracts of property. It was not a city like setting at all. But rather there were people, dwellings and some business related structures scattered about the countryside. There were as well many other large areas of woods here and there. But nevertheless here in their very midst were these two monsters roaming around. Why it was inconceivable to both of us what had just transpired. So we left having found our greatest piece to date for our collection. And having had the greatest encounter imaginable to mankind as well. We will never forget it. Before we left for home we had contacted and stopped by the Tyler's to talk over the events. They told us over coffee and cake that such things were heard of in Oregon but never did they put any real credence into the stories when they were told to them. And so there you have it my dear reader. Once again people who have seen something because they are looking for something. I think the biblical narrative says seek and you shall find. And sometimes it seems like you may find something other than what you were seeking. Or perhaps in this case. Both!

✗

The Vancouver Evidence

I thought it worthy of inclusion within this book. An evidentiary story which was given first hand from an uncle to a nephew. Having occurred in the deep woods of Vancouver. From here on out you will be reading Reggie LeCarres testimony. I was born and raised in the Vancouver area. In college I had achieved a degree in electrical engineering and found myself working for a startup company in Spokane Washington. It was here that I made friends with a coworker named Clifford Wells from Pennsylvania. He too was an engineer. During one of our many dinners together and after having had a brew or two. We overheard some characters at the bar shouting and laughing with each other about Bigfoot. At some point I said to Cliffy. What do you think about Bigfoot? Is it real or not? And after Cliffy had tried to make some lofty and well thought out comments. I reached into my wallet and pulled out a picture. It was a still shot of the famous Patty picture if I am correct with the name and I passed it to Cliff. He immediately said oh I've seen this before. This is a still shot of that cowboy's film clip supposedly taken in the woods somewhere back in the fifties. I told him that my uncle had given this to me when I was young. And he gave it to me with a warning. The warning being to always carry more gun than you think you need when you go in the woods. And the picture being a reminder to me of why I should do so.

Now Cliff and I went back and forth a little about the photograph while we consumed a few more brews. And I told him that according to what my uncle had told me. He and his logging crew were actually run off a job by these things many years ago up in the Canadian woods. Cliff had asked me if my uncle was still alive to which I said yes. And then he asked me if it was possible that we could go see him? I would really like to talk to him about what he and the men experienced. I think it would be kind of cool to hear it firsthand. So I told him absolutely. He would love to see me and meet you as well. He's a really cool old woodsman. It was arranged during a little summer vacation around the 4th of July that he and I would go and visit my Uncle Frank. We found ourselves sitting in Uncle Frank's modest home and chatting it up about what I had shown and told Cliff. At some point Uncle Frank said to us. Hey listen fellas. If you'd like to we can go up to the old logging site. And if they are still there I can show you some really weird stuff. Now who doesn't like to see weird stuff? So the next day we took off in his truck. It's actually quite funny because my uncle never invited me to see anything. Neither had he mentioned the availability of seeing any weird stuff as he called it. But all things happen for a reason.

And here we were with Uncle Frank about to zero in on seeing some weird things as he called them. We drove for about 90 minutes to a break in the woods where he turned off the road and we started up a wide dirt road onto a hill or low mountainside. I thought the suspension was going to fall out from under us. And thankfully it wasn't until we were almost where he wanted to bring us. That the trail was so rutted it became impassable.

So we got out and walked. I think we must have walked for a mile on what was a fairly steep incline. Now Uncle Frank was 76 years old but he could arm wrestle a bear still being in very good shape. We got to a flat topped area which I think he called the stage or landing. Something like that I really don't remember. He told us that many times they were hired to clear out hillsides where severe wind storms had downed allot of trees. These locations I think he said were what they called windfall. They would create a flat work area above where the trees were that needed to be taken. From there they would place some type of machine with a big boom on it. From which a thick cable of some sort would be run down to the base of the hillside by the crew. The cable would be secured to the top of a large tree at the bottom of the hill. This would create somewhat of a cable tightrope from the bottom to the top of the work area. The men would work down the hill trimming up the trees that were knocked down. And cutting down all of the other trees which still remained standing. Trees which they would then wrap a choker of cable around in bunches. This cable was attached to a hoist or trolley of some kind which was suspended from the overhead cable. The overhead trolley would then lift and pull the trees back up the hill to the staging area.

As we looked the area over the place was a mess. It looked like a large bomb had gone off leveling everything. There was quite a bit of new growth there that had taken over through the years. But the evidence of the work that these men had performed was still present so many years later. After a while he said to us. Now I can't go with you I'm much too old for this crap. But if you can navigate your way down over in that direction. You will come across some old oil and fuel drums. Take a good look at them and when you come back we will have a talk about what you have seen. He told us to go slow and watch your step that you don't sprain an ankle or worse. It was like walking through and over a plate of spaghetti. Only the spaghetti was made of tree branches, brush and debris.

When they so called cleared an area. They really didn't clear it at all. They strictly took the money lumber and everything else was left behind like a junk heap. Finally we reached an area where we could see some drums that were old, rusty and crushed. Well he told us to look them over and so we did. All of the drums were still sealed and appeared to be relatively full with the exception of some of the tops. Where the welds or crimps on the drums were rusting out. Most of the other tops and bottoms of the drums were still fully intact. But the tops and bottoms of each drum were bulging outward like pressure from within had forced them out. An expansion if you will. And all of the screw caps were in place and still sealed up. And now for the weirdness.

Each of the drums of which there were nine. Were cinched or squeezed in around the middle. Similar to the shape of an hour glass. And upon closer inspection there was no indication to our eyes of a chain or anything else having been placed around them to cause this to happen. There were no visible scratches or grooves in the metal. And many of them had a good amount of paint still on them. These were industrial 50 gallon steel drums. And you could still smell diesel, gasoline and oil all around them in the area. If he hadn't told us where to go I don't believe that anyone else could have found them.

Many were wedged in piles of branches and debris. Having thought to ourselves that we had done our due diligence. Being instructed to look carefully at them by Uncle Frank. We climbed back up to this landing area. What a freaking ordeal that was. Coming down was one thing but getting back up was quite another.

And his crew had to deal with this stuff every single day. These men must have been animals. When we had reached the top completely winded from the climb Uncle Frank laughed at us. He said to the two of us you guys are wimps. So tell me what exactly did you see down there? I want to hear all about it. So we told him about all of the things that we have just told you. And then he told us to take seat. He told us that he and his crew of seven men had come to this site in the usual way. They had everything set to begin working and had begun to go about their business.

The 50 gallon drums were kept on the staging area. They contained lubricant, grease, diesel and gasoline. Everything that the machinery needed to operate. It was a large tract of timber and they would be there for a quite a while clearing it out. Having arrived back to the job site on the morning of the second day. There had been some damage done to the equipment overnight. Odd things were just broken, smashed or twisted around. Similar to what you would find in an act of pure vandalism. It was so bad that they could not even begin to work until many of the things were fixed. And many of the things required that they had to leave the job going back into town to bring back those things which would be needed to render the repairs.

They were already losing money because no work was being done cutting down the timber. After the second day the same thing happened. We came back to the site in the morning only to see much of the equipment damaged again. In fact some of the things we had just fixed were broken in the same way as the day before. The owner who was also a worker was furious. He was cursing and accusing a rival in the industry of sabotaging the jobsite. I mean this guy was going nuts. I said to myself if the other guy had been there be he guilty or not. It would have been bloodshed for sure. And sometimes these dudes would come to each other's jobs just to bust each other's chops.

It was not a good relationship by any means between these different crews. It was more of a rivalry. And so knowing full well that the accusations may actually have been well founded. The boss then having had his fill of two days of this crap decided to put an armed guard at the site every night. He actually grabbed two characters from a local gin mill. He paid a 100 bucks a night for the pair of them to stay at the site with their rifles until morning every day. This went on for about a week. Every night they built a big fire and sat there until the morning.

And nothing else happened on the site after they were posted there. We worked with no extraordinary issues each day for that entire week. Finally the boss was tired of shelling out a hundred a day and told them they wouldn't be needed anymore. He figured whoever had been doing the damage would not waste their time anymore coming to the site knowing that there were guards waiting there. Guards who may very well shoot them.

The very next day following no fire being made overnight. And no guards with rifles watching the site. We came into the job in the morning and all of the supply drums were gone. Of which at the time there were five. And so in a rage he left the site and returned with four more drums. That very night he decided to stay there himself. This time he was not going to light a fire. He was going to sit quietly in the cab of the crane with his shotgun and whoever showed up was going to get a belly full of lead. Well the next morning when the crew arrived the boss was nowhere to be found. The door was opened on the cab. The handle had been torn from the door and the catch latch was damaged on the frame of the cab.

We searched for him for hours and hours shouting his name throughout the woods. Up and down the hill scouring every square inch as best as we could. The only thing that we found was his 12 gauge about a 100 feet from the cab which was bent in half like in a Superman episode. Finally one of the guys went back to town to get the police. That day and the days following a massive search was done of the area in an effort to find him.

They never found his body. Only his hat was retrieved from out in the timber. And the four drums he had just brought to the jobsite that day. They were found by the search team in the same area as the five from the previous day's disappearance. In the same fashion and condition as you boys had just seen them. Squeezed around the middle and thrown clear down the hill.

My Uncle was right. These drums were not rolled down the hill. They couldn't have made it 10 feet without falling into the large branches and debris. Something had picked these drums up weighing hundreds of pounds apiece. Crushed them around the middle and hurled them some 80 feet away. What the hell has the power to do such a thing? And that's why I gave you the picture and the warning. For no human being or beings could have done such a thing in my opinion. To this very day the boss is still listed as a missing person. And as far as I know among the locals. No further talk or consideration was given to the crushed drums or the bent shotgun that was found. Something was not happy about us being in their neighborhood. That's for damn sure!

✗

The Great Divide Trail Encounter

Dave Sorenson and Mike Ruddick were heading off to Jasper National Park in the summer of 1987. The two of them were both Ironman competitors having come to the park from the Pittsburg Pennsylvania area. They had struck up a lifelong friendship having met each other at various competitions in the region. Being competitive swimmers, runners and bikers their friendship evolved into taking hiking trips together annually and this was one of those trips. For those of you who may not know Jasper National Park is located in Alberta Canada.

We say here in the states that everything's bigger in Texas. Well we will see about that. Dave and Mike were both present for my interview and so from here on out it will be the two of them telling their story. Mike and I like to pick unusual and out of the way places whenever possible for our annual hikes. We are not always looking for the greatest challenge to us physically but we don't shy away from that either. We picked for this trip the largest national park in the Canadian Rockies. No matter how you slice it this place is wild country and the park itself is particularly interesting. It is has within its borders some of the most beautiful rivers and snowcapped mountainous areas that you will ever set eyes upon.

One of the most beautiful lakes that you will ever see. And some alpine meadow areas which I thought only existed in Switzerland. It also has an abundance of wildlife such as bears, moose and elk. I will also warn any of your readers that if you go there be especially careful in the mornings and at dusk when driving. For if you choose not to heed my warning you do so at your own peril.

Another of the things that attracted us to this area was that you can actually stay in the town of Jasper. Being able to drive from there by car into many access areas of the park. There are in excess of 600 miles of trails within the parks boundaries. And I was told that most of them were initially game trails. We flew into Calgary International Airport and rented a car. The transition was sweet and easy. There are a number of lodge accommodations located within the vicinity of the park as well as horse outfitters and guide services for those who are interested in such things. It's really quite a nice and well thought out operation within and without of the park. And none of this takes away in the slightest from what we came there for which was to get away and experience the wild country. The human footprint here is virtually unrecognizable.

On our first day in town we wasted no time. We had seen a tram going up a mountainside and decided to check it out. This Jasper Tramway as it's called takes you up the side of Whistlers Mountain to an elevation of about 7500 feet. There is a tour guide with you for what amounts to be about a 10 minute ride which is incredible to say the least. At the top there are boardwalks and trails to walk on and have a look around.

From there we were told that we were actually seeing 6 other mountain ranges as well as the Athabasca River and some glacial lakes. It was out of this world and I highly recommend it. For our first days hike we had selected what's known as the Great Divide Trail. It was rated as being hard which is fine for us. We took Maligne Lake Road from Jasper to the northern corner of Maligne Lake. The day that we went there some low level wispy clouds were floating over the valley. They actually looked like pieces of drawn out cotton drifting overhead. Snow covered mountain peaks which are visible in every direction that you turn are due to the park being situated on the western side of the Rockies. It would be very difficult to get lost in here because the mountains are always in view and alongside of you. The lake itself I believe is about 14 or 15 miles long and there are trails that can be followed the entire length on both sides. And many other side trails to take you anywhere you are willing to venture.

So on our first day we decided to begin on a trail that was somewhat hugging the lake. After which the trail meanders out into a heavily forested area. As I said earlier this is wild country. So when I say a trail we are talking about animal footpaths. These are not wide car of truck paths. The terrain at times can be very rough and rocky making it extremely arduous. We were going to head somewhat southeast from where we began and at some point we would stop to rest to eat. After which we would begin to make our way back out. The two of us generally like to familiarize ourselves with areas before we go full bore into them when we hike. I think many novice hikers get into trouble by not putting into practice such things. The tendency being to bite off more of a hike than they can chew so to speak.

There was an abundance of wildlife in here. We did see a number of elk as well as quite a few smaller critters. This park has a very diverse and unique ecosystem. And so our first days hike in and out began and ended in about 6 or 7 hours. And believe me it was quite a workout to complete. After spending a relaxing night in town conversing with some of the locals and chowing down. We made plans for the next day. It was decided on by the two of us to begin in the same area only this time in we would take a slightly more westerly approach. This was a deeply timbered and rocky terrain which looked like it would push our limits physically.

By the way when you are hiking in a group or in this case two people. Always carry two compasses each being held by a different person. In this way if something happens to the one of the compasses. In other words if one breaks or is lost you always have a backup. Always try to keep visual markers of where you have come from and where you are heading whenever possible. This can be extremely difficult in heavily forested hikes and this is how people get lost. In our situation here we were going in and out of large stands of spruce and fir trees. So it was relatively easy to keep our bearings as we went along. Moving along on the trail we had just passed through a beautiful meadow comprised of tall wheat like grasses and an abundance of wild flowers.

I guess we were about 2 hours into the hike when we began entering into yet another stand of trees. This stand was fairly dense and growing relatively close together. You couldn't see clearly for any great distance and yet at times there were what I will call bowling alley or lane type views available for a couple of hundred feet. As we were approaching one such area I waved to my partner to stop and be quiet. I had seen something moving that was reddish brown and my first thought was it's a grizzly bear. As we stood side by side very still .

I pulled my field glasses up to my eyes. It was no grizzly bear. There was a large felled tree lying on the ground which I could plainly see was in the state of decay. I quickly realized that what I was seeing was in a straddling position over the tree. And just as I was coming to grips with what I was looking at Mike shouts out…Go Bear! Go Bear! What a mistake this was. Of course he wasn't seeing what I was looking at through the binoculars. This thing that was straddling the log jumped up and turned in one fluid movement. It took about two quick steps towards us and flexing its body lifted its head into the air like a wolf letting out what can only be described as an earth shattering scream. It was part scream and part roar if you can wrap your head around that. It then stared at us kind of grunting. About 10 seconds later it reached down and grabbed a piece of tree limb hurling it towards us. This was followed by yet another blood curdling howl. I said to myself that everyone and anything in the park must have heard it. The sound was so powerful that it sent reverberations through my entire body. It was at that moment that I realized the futility of carrying bear spray and not a gun.

There was no way that I would want this thing or anything for that matter to get close enough to me for the spray to be effective. If I had a gun I would have already been shooting at it of that I can assure you. This was no man and it was no bear. It was a monster. I saw Mike's hands shaking. The monster was well over 10 feet tall and as nuts as it may sound it really appeared to be closer to 14 feet tall. We have been close to bull elk. And in Yellowstone we were not far from large grazing buffalo. I am telling you flat out. No bullshit! This thing must have easily been 2000 lbs. It started rolling its head around like a weight lifter trying to get loose. At the same time it was swiping its arms back and forth in the air. And every few seconds a loud grunt or growl would emanate from it. And as if things couldn't get any worse the beast took about 3 or 4 more rapid steps towards us and stopped. It was like a short sprint after which he stopped abruptly snarling at us. To me it was an intimidation move in an attempt to back us down and show us that he was the boss. It sounds stupid but I could see a penis and that's why I said he.

Now my own chest is a 52. I wear a 2x in everything I buy. This monsters chest must have been a 200x. It looked like a living bulldozer with gigantic hands, arms and legs. And the speed with which it was able to move during the short burst told me that if it was going to really charge us it could have been on top of us in seconds and that would be the end of us. And then suddenly in the distance we heard another howling noise which seemed to get this creatures attention. It was prolonged and loud. He then turned his attention once again to us presenting us with a grimace which showed us its teeth. And then it slowly turned and walked away. And as it did so it craned its neck looking at us several times and it was gone.

The two of us dropped our packs and sat down. I felt like every ounce of energy had left my body. We were in shock. I said to Mike that when I put the binoculars on it before he yelled… Go Bear! And all hell broke loose. I knew it wasn't a bear. I could see an arm going to the face and I could clearly see a leg bent like a human being alongside of the log. We must have been holding our breath during the encounter because we both were breathing heavy and panting.

A little while later we walked over where it had been sitting. We could see that it was digging in the rotten log. There were fat white larvae in the decaying matter. And there were a couple of large leaves from some type of plant lying next to the log with a bunch of these larvae lying on top of them. This was like a dinner plate. This thing was gathering food and eating when we interrupted it. No wonder it was pissed off. The log where it was sitting smelled like shit. I mean it wreaked. And you could see how it was ripping the log apart to expose the rotten interior. There were a few large prints around the area which were clearly visible and the impressions were very deep. I put my forefinger into one and it came up to the middle knuckle. Now I wear a size 10 E and these prints were more than double mine with my hiking boots on. And that's in length and width. Mike and I had been on many hikes together around North America. We had seen and experienced a great deal of wildlife together.

We had both heard many of the stories of Bigfoot and had talked about them often. I guess both of us were of the mindset that we will believe it when we see it. Well now we were believers because we had just seen it. We never again went into the woods without a gun. It was at this point that I asked Dave to expound on any descriptive details of the creature which he may have left out and here is what he said. Thinking back on what I said about the log smelling like shit. When it was walking away you could see that its butt areas fur was all crusted and matted together. There was allot of something sticking to the fur. From the side view. That is from its front to the back of its rump. It must have been 3 feet thick. And I would say shoulder to shoulder all of 6 feet easy. Its muscles no matter which group we are speaking of were such as nothing you have ever seen on earth. They were exponentially 10, 20 or 30 times the size of a humans. What I mean to say is there is no chart to measure these things. It's like saying an oak tree is its arm and the twig is mine. Absolutely ridiculous in dimensions and proportions. I think that this creature could have pulled over a rooted tree. That's how strong it looked. When it grimaced at us I could see longer fang teeth. Not like a tigers but longer than the rest in its mouth. Which said to me that this thing eats meat. And from the stink of its shit it had been eating some meat.

Thank God we weren't its next feast. The hair was long and scraggly and its jaw kind of protruded from its face. The mouth area was massive when it howled. You could have put a cantaloupe in there with no problem whatsoever. I said its hair because it wasn't like normal animal fur. It wasn't dense and short. You could see some of its body through the hair which made me wonder how they stay warm. Because as you know when the weather gets colder an animals fur typically thickens. But who's to say how these beasts were created. They are a complete and utter enigma to mankind. People just will not believe they are real until one of them try's to rip you a new asshole. Then everything changes and quickly.

✗

The Yellowstone Scouting Encounter

This is the story of Hector Rodríguezes encounter in Yellowstone Park. Whoever said that the Boy Scouts wasn't a fun organization to join? From here on out will be Hectors recollection of the August encounter. Well it's as I already told you Bill when we first spoke. I was retired N.Y.P.D. when I got involved with the Scouts. I had actually been a scout myself when I was a young boy. I should say that I was a Cub and a Weblo. Because by the time I was ready for full blown Boy Scouts things didn't work out in my family at that time for me to continue on.

Our troop was in the Boroughs of N.Y.C. Which is not much of a place for Scouting but it's better than the streets if you catch my drift. Many of the young boys had a rough life. Some came from families that didn't have a pot to piss in. I and some of the other men were always ponying up cash to help the kids out. If you can believe it some of the boys had never seen a beach or been out of their Borough so much as one time in their entire life. Such is the life of many inner city youths. Well anyway the leaders and I had gotten together on planning a trip. Something that would be geared around Scouting and vacationing.

When we unveiled our plan to the boys they went nuts. Our plan was to be a year out in the making and we were going to go to Yellowstone. Now these kids for the most part could not count on family money to fund the trip and we knew that. So we had the boys do some fund raisers in their churches. As well as going to local businesses pounding the bricks for some cash. They actually did quite well. And as was always the case I and the other men kicked in about 5 grand in total to supplement the rest that was needed. We had planned ahead and made reservations for two cabins right near the park.

There were four adults and nine boys in total. It would be tight but nobody cared. For them and myself this would be the trip of a lifetime. The furthest I had been from home was a charter fishing trip in Montauk Point Long Island. I was still very much like these little guys at 51 years of age.

The fishing charter was a morning that I will never forget. The cost was 250 bucks per man times 6 of us for a full day charter boat. We had made a side bet for the day amongst ourselves. Whoever caught the biggest Striper would go for free. And as fate would have it that would be me. I reeled in a 47 pound cow on a live herring. It was a great day and I knew in my heart that this trip would provide good and lasting memories for these boys as well. They were a great bunch of young people who were proud of being Boy Scouts. And so the day came that all the pieces had finally come together and we arrived at the cabins.

The cabins were really cool and the boys already were grinning from ear to ear. Imagine yourself never having seen anything but concrete and cars and now you are in this location. It was the beginning of something that I didn't want to end for them or for me. Our agenda was to do a little of everything which for the most part in the park involves allot of walking. But we were up to it and so were the boys. Wild horses could not have slowed them down. We were if I recall correctly on our fourth day in the park when we had scoped out a fairly rigorous trail that would ascend quite high up the side of a mountain.

Three of the men were at the head of the pack and I was trailing behind. The boys being in the middle as we began the hike. We had reached an area where we were hugging the side of a rock wall as we walked and there was a steep hillside sloping off and down to our left side. This hillside was covered with some very dense forest that was comprised of a great deal of smaller and larger pine trees. As well as the tops of some other trees which were growing much further below us peeking out of the top. Having made it up to about as high as we would go. Which by the way was nowhere near the end of this trail. We stopped for a refreshment break after which we started heading back down. We had been walking for about two hours to reach the point where we had stopped. It was then as we began our descent that something was pinching my foot inside of my boot. So I stopped to take my shoe off not saying anything to the others who kept on walking. Don't ask me why that's just what happened. I guess at the time I thought it would take me a minute and I would scurry to catch up with them. When I looked up they were out of my sight having already gone around a bend in the trail and I couldn't hear their voices anymore. Now all I had on me was a large knife and two of the other men had bear spray. As I was putting the boot back on the tops of several trees off to my right side started to shake violently. Kind of like a cheerleaders pompoms.

I remember saying to myself what the hell is that? And a few seconds later from the side of the wooded slope emerged a large apelike monster. A creature which stood up directly in front of me blocking not only the trail but my being able to descend on it as well. I saw it coming out of the brush on all fours. But upon reaching the trail it immediately stood up on two legs just like a human. It was basically the same height as me which is a little over 6 feet tall. But it must have weighed 700 pounds and its body was like a block of muscles. The creatures face was kind of like a humans. But what I really mean to say is that it didn't look like a gorilla. It was sort of like a hybrid face if that makes any sense to you. And it just stood there. It was moving its head around in a weird way while not really focusing its eyes on me. It kept opening and shutting its mouth and kind of stretching its jaws at the same time. And all of this while not making a sound.

Then it started to swat the branches that were next to it. I didn't want to shout for fear that I would startle it. Frankly I didn't know what to do. So I started to slowly backtrack up the trail hoping it would go back down the slope but it didn't. This thing starts to follow me up the trail. Now all I could think was could I beat it off if it came down to an attack? So I withdrew my knife when suddenly I could hear the boys and men calling my name. From the sounds of their voices they were obviously getting closer not knowing what they were walking into. As their voices could be heard getting louder and louder this thing started shaking and twitching like a crack addict. And with one quick hop it leaped off the trail back down the slope. I could see some trees moving and could hear it going down the side of the embankment. I started walking towards the group and felt safe enough to call out to them. When we met up of course they all started saying the usual stuff. Where were you? Why didn't you tell us to stop? We thought you got hurt. All I said to them was that something was hurting my foot and I had stopped to take my boot off. I said nothing of what had happened during the 5 minute encounter because I didn't want to scare the boys. That night when the boys had all nodded off. I and the guys were having a couple of beers when I told them what had happened on the trail after I stopped to remove my boot. John said to me I knew that something was up when I looked at your face. You looked as white as a ghost. They were as baffled hearing about what transpired as I was experiencing it. At any rate that's how it started and ended. The boys to this day have never heard a word about it. In fact one of the boys is about to retire from the N.Y.P.D. himself. Time really flies.

And as I always do I asked Hector to embellish on the description of the creature and here is what he said. Well its head was slightly cone shaped. Not to a point but not rounded like a man's either. I was less than 15 feet away from this thing. It had allot of hair on it but it was not entirely covered like a bear or a dog. And the hair was longer in length. I guess in some areas 8 or 10 inches. It did stink a little kind of like a locker room after a workout. It looked really nervous because its movements were really jerky and abrupt. It also up to the point it left me made no sudden movement towards me. But who knows what may have happened if the circumstances were different. It was built like some kind of superhuman lineman. It had virtually no waist line and was like a wide cube of muscles. The arms were extremely long and thick and I could see the individual muscles even through the fur. And its hands when it wasn't moving were a full length below its knees. The eyes were as black as an eight ball and very shiny. But very deeply recessed in its head. It had an extremely large jaw that jutted out at the chin which reminded me of an old cartoon character named Gigantor the Space-Age Robot. When it walked it wasn't like a monkey or a chimp. This thing walked like you and me. Virtually straight up except for a slight hunch to its posture. Its head was actually leaning forward of its shoulders. I think that initially when I saw it emerge it was climbing up the side like we would. Using its hands and feet for grip. Well that's about all I can say. It was absolutely astonishing.

✗

The Stone Mountain Sighting

Ricky Stegmeir was part of a team that was to film a group of climbers at Stone Mountain North Carolina. From this point forward it will be Ricky telling the story of what happened to him and the other cameramen that day by the side of Stone Mountain. I was part of a photography class in college. I should clarify that I am not talking about still photography. What I am speaking about is motion picture filming.

One day in class while waiting for it to begin. A fellow student started showing us some stills he had shot of a group of rock climbers by Stone Mountain. He was going on and on about the climbers ascending the shear rock face and the intensity he had felt while watching them do what they do. He thought that this would be a great opportunity and location to shoot some live action footage. Now there was a small group of us who were of like mind in the class. And after some discussion we were in agreement that this would in fact be a great opportunity for us to cut our teeth and show our skills in live filming. And so over a period of a few weeks we further discussed the particulars of what we would do and how we would accomplish it. The only obstacle was that none of us were climbers. So a couple of the guys took upon themselves the task of finding some climbers who would be willing to do the climb under our direction. This actually turned out to be quite simple. We were easily able to find some locals after we had spread the word who were more than happy to assist us in our effort. Stone Mountain is a 600 foot tall granite outcropping. It is said to have formed over 300 million years ago when magma forced its way upward through the earth's crust.

This upheaval formed an approximately 25 square mile area of igneous rock which today forms the edge of North Carolinas mountain range. The sides of Stone Mountain have been deeply grooved over millions of years by water running down its sides from the top. These grooves appear like deep wrinkles in the otherwise smooth surface of the domes face. After a few weeks had passed since we committed ourselves to the project.

We met and teamed up with a couple of climbers. In actuality it was three individuals. Two guys and a woman. We decided that we would go to the dome as a group in order to scope out the area for anything worthwhile to film. As well as preparing ourselves mentally for where we would set up for the shoot. We also needed to figure out just what type of equipment would be best suited for the work. The climbers told us that there was a trail called the Stone Mountain Loop which may be of some interest to us. They also said that it was quite treacherous and not for the faint of heart. Now when you start talking treacherous you are talking about a great filming opportunity. So we all bought in without a hitch. The following week we got together for a hike where we were immediately confronted with some formidable warning signs. Dig this man. *THIS AREA CONTAINS HAZARDS ASSOCIATED WITH ROCKS STEEP SLOPES AND CLIFFS…INJURY OR DEATH IS POSSIBLE…STAY ON THE MARKED TRAIL!*

Now I can only speak for myself but that is quite the warning. Nobody had said anything about potentially dying today. And so having read the sign and understood the potential ramifications we commenced the hike. The trail begins going up and up and did I say up? At this point of the trail you are ascending through the forest. And when you finally break out you find yourself in an immense field of gigantic flat pieces or slabs of granite. According to my pedometer we had climbed about one mile. From this vantage point there were absolutely magnificent views as far as the eye could see. It was simply breathtaking.

Our mountaineer buddy's told us that if we were to continue on the trail we would be in for a real treat. And so on their lead we did continue. A short while later we were approaching Stone Mountain Falls. Which is a waterfall descending some two or three hundred feet from the top of the dome. It was an absolutely fantastic sensory experience. There is a grouping of boardwalks from which you can get a real good view of the falls. And then the descent brings you right back down to the base of the dome.

As you are descending the trail passes through the trees once again overlooking a large meadow. It was here as we were coming down and looking out over the meadow that we could see a fairly large herd of deer grazing within the meadow itself. And so having somewhat circumnavigated the dome in a manner of speaking. We put our cooperative heads together in order to devise the best plan for positioning ourselves to film the climbers on the face of the wall. Two days later we had beautiful weather as the team approached the base of the dome. We had three cameras and the three climbers. I was to position myself over towards the meadow. Bobby was on the other side of the climbers. And Roberta was at the base filming from a straight on position. We had several walkie-talkies with which to communicate our actions to each other.

The climbers began their ascent and I tell you no lie that I was in fear of their imminent death the entire time. How anybody could stay clinging to that rock face for such a long time is beyond me. I don't know where they get the strength and stamina from. It was beyond words especially for the climber who takes the lead. The reality was that they were making incredible time. Like a well-oiled machine the three of them went skyward. And finally they were at the top waving at us and cheering. From my perspective everything had gone superbly well. And I knew that we had taken some great film of their ascent. It was so exciting for all of us.

After a brief rest the climbers began to repel back down the face. I was standing there filming when I heard some commotion off to my left in the meadow. And I have to say to you that for the most part we were virtually silent the majority of the time with the exception of a few brief moments on the radios. I heard what sounded like some type of animal sound like a squeal for lack of a better word. It was coming from out in the meadow.

As I turned my head I saw what appeared to be a large kind of arching hump of brown color in the meadow. It looked like a brown lump of fur protruding over the top of the grass. It was then that

I realized that the hump was moving up and down. It looked like something brown was bent over and moving up and down over something else. I hope I am doing a good job of explaining this but it was very weird. Whatever it was had the appearance of someone pulling weeds out of the ground with both hands.

Moments later this thing that I knew immediately was a Bigfoot stood up. It had a large lifeless deer under its arm. From my perspective and at quite a distance I didn't know how tall the grass was out there or how far the distance was that I was looking at. But as an estimate I would have to say that most of the field was about three feet or so high. And it appeared to be up to somewhere around the mid-thigh or groin area of the Bigfoot. I would estimate that it was somewhere between 7 and 9 feet tall and extremely broad at the back and shoulders. It must have been 200 yards or less away from my position. As crazy as it sounds I could still see some of the deer in the meadow not too far away from what I was seeing. They were maybe forty of fifty yards away from the kill. I thought that this was kind of odd but then I recalled when watching an African documentary. How the gazelles hung around after the lions had culled one of them out.

All of this took about 45 seconds from first glance. I don't know if this thing had stalked them crawling through the weeds or what. I wondered also if maybe it hadn't seen me. Which if it was crawling down in the grass it wouldn't have. And even though I wasn't moving or making any noise so to speak. In my mind I thought that it should have smelled me at the very least. At any rate it started to walk away from my position very quickly with the deer under its arm. I turned to grab the tripod and camera in order to position it for some footage of the beast. And when I did so with the adrenalin pumping a hundred miles an hour through my veins. I had knocked the whole tripod and camera to the ground. By the time I picked it up and tried to reposition everything to film and checking that nothing was broken,

The monster was already in the tree line and completely obscured from my view. It was then that I grabbed my radio and started telling the others frantically what had just transpired. But we had to keep filming. We had spent the whole day at the base of the rock wall and couldn't stop now. As the climb ended and we all gathered together the climbers were now part of the conversation about the Bigfoot. They had seen nothing. Their eyes being transfixed on each other and the rock face the entire time. It's too bad because they would really have had a bird's eye view of the whole event.

Well the rest is history as they say. That was my Bigfoot sighting. And as is always the case I asked Rick to embellish on any of the Bigfoots features and here is what he said. The creature appeared to be reddish brown in color. And its hair was relatively speaking long.

The head in particular had much longer hair than the rest of the body that I could see. Its side and back was to me the entire time so I never got a chance to see the face. But it was truly huge and very well built. It walked entirely upright just like we do. I couldn't see anything from about the crotch and lower because of the grass. But its strength was obvious in that it was cradling this large deer in one hand. Like you or I would hold a football. And that same arm was actually swinging a bit while it walked. It appeared to be effortless for this thing. I mean think about it for a minute. Loping away in the field with a deer in your hand. Let's just say it was 125 or 150 lbs. That's unbelievable. The whole thing is unbelievable! Its head seemed to melt right into its shoulders. In other words there wasn't any neck. And the muscles in its buttocks were incredibly pronounced.

✗

The Strawberry Lake Trail 5 Sighting

The following is a sighting which was told to me by Marilyn Sorenson a resident of the state of Montana. Here are the details of the sighting according to Marilyn's testimony. The Strawberry Lake Trail Number 5 is about 6 miles in and out. It ends near the Jewel Basin at Strawberry Lake where you can then pick up on Alpine Trail Number 7 if you are an ambitious enough hiker desirous to extend your day's journey. As trails go it is not a very long hike and it is also a multi-use trail. Which means you can run into people on horseback and even mountain bikes.

I belong to a very informal group or club of hikers. We have no name for the group being simply people of like mind and spirit who enjoy hiking and taking in all that nature has to offer us. Now if you have never been in my home state. There are a ridiculous amount of gorgeous hiking venues. And in the past 17 years or so I have been on more than a few of them. It is some really fine country. This particular trail has a fair amount of elevation change and quite a few switchbacks as trails go. It was a Thursday morning in early September when I and two other ladies began the hike to Strawberry Lake. Now just to give you a heads up about this area. The trail in most locations and in particular when you are walking along a hillside can be extremely narrow. In other words the low brush is literally rubbing against your legs. So shorts are not advisable.

There is visible bear scat throughout the entire hike. Which of course means that there is an ample supply of bears who provided the scat. And with all the switchbacks and dense brush it is the perfect place to stumble upon something which you may not want to. This was actually my third hike on this trail and on the last trip I saw a black bear eating some huckleberries. And when I told her to scoot she ran like the wind. The fact being that bears really don't want anything to do with us. It's when you startle them or come upon a sow with cubs that the trouble begins. This has never happened to me or anyone that I know. The trail ends at Strawberry Lake which is really in my opinion nothing more than a large beautiful pond that is breathtaking none the less. And many hikers in season go for a dip in the lake midway through their hike. You are hiking in here through what I would call foot hills. They are not large and we are talking hundreds of feet of elevation for the most part.

But there are however some mountains surrounding you up to about 5 thousand feet. What I am trying to impress on you is that you are not dealing with allot of elevation during the hike itself. Having said that along the denser and narrower areas of the trail it is flanked with huge patches of huckleberries and raspberries hence all the bears. And the abundance of berries can make for some great snacking for us humans as well. You are typically walking on the side of one hill which means that you are looking at the sides of some other hills as you walk. And so not to confuse you the trail is not all dense underbrush. It is also comprised of some heavily forested areas. I am talking about tightly packed stands of pines. In other locations the view is of patches of pines which are growing here and there within some reddish brown twiggy undergrowth that covers the majority of the visible slopes. In these areas the dark green contrast of the trees against the slopes is quite dramatic. In many spots on the trail you walk into grand open vistas comprised of large sloping grassy hillsides descending to the bottom. There are wildflowers in abundance and it is some of the most scenic country in the world. So we had made it up to Strawberry Lake in a couple of hours which included numerous stops to take in the views as well as getting our fill of the berries.

The area next to the lake in one spot although I would not call it a beach. Is kind of a hard pack with some pea gravel mixed in and there are hills surrounding the lake which are stacked with tall pointed pines. It must have been about a half hour later having sat and rested that we started heading back. It was at about the midway point of our return trek that an adjoining hill or mountainside comes into view. And you are looking at it for quite a while in your peripheral vision while you are walking along. This area was as I mentioned before comprised of patches of dark green pines amidst this reddish brown undergrowth. The only reason I mention this is that unless something was walking in the patches of trees. It would stand out like a sore thumb against the lighter colored backdrop of the undergrowth. It was only moments after we had rounded this bend which opened up into the view I just spoke of. That my girlfriend pointed and said to us. Hey you guys look at that! On the opposite side about midway up the slope we could clearly see three creatures. At first glance I thought we were looking at bears. But within seconds I could tell that one was sitting and the other two were standing. And I am talking about on two legs. We all crouched down and remained still even though we were very far away from them. They were very darkly colored. Much darker than anything else that was distinguishable to the eye.

As we watched them with great intent the two smaller ones appeared to be wrestling. Like two little Roman Greco wrestlers. They would oppose each other and then run in and grapple. We could clearly see arms extended towards each other as they kept doing this over and over. Breaking and grappling. Breaking and grappling. Every so often they would go to the larger sitting one for a few moments. We all said to each other that these are Bigfoot. It was obvious to us that it was two youths playing with their father or mother watching them. What else could it be? A father and two children dressed in gorilla suits in the middle of nowhere. We stayed there for the better part of an hour watching them. They were playing and taking little breathers in-between. At some point they got up and walked away out of our field of view. When they started walking it was then that we could see the larger one in all of its glory. We were sharing a small pair of Zeiss binoculars but at this distance they were of very little help. They were so small they could fit in the palm of your hand. The larger one when they stood and started walking was visibly at least three times larger than the two smaller ones. The difference being like that of an adult elk standing with a newborn calve.

The adult was massive in its proportions to the others as well. We just couldn't see any other details other than a very long arm length and swing. And they had a very methodical and steady stride as they walked. It was clear that the bigger one was taking very long steps pausing at times to allow the little ones to catch up. Just as we would when walking with a small child. It was really remarkable to have the privilege of seeing this. I have personally seen in all likelihood 50 bears in my life. I have seen innumerable elk as well as herds of bison and wild horses. And I have even come fairly close to a mountain lion. But this really took the cake. To think that we had seen three Bigfoot in the wild and for such a long time was really quite the experience. And it wasn't only seeing them that was exciting. But it was watching them in the act of what they were doing. They were obviously a family out for a stroll and getting in some play time in as well.

I didn't bother asking Marilyn for any additional details. For it was obvious during the interview that the distance was too great for anything more to be seen by the women.

Missing Person Washington State

This account was told to me by Butch McCaskey. It is he from this point forward who will be telling his own story. At the time of this event I was living in Redmond Washington. And my co-worker Paul was living in Seattle. The two of us were involved in the food service industry. We actually owned a business together which we operated in Seattle. Paul was born and bred in the state and I was a transplant from Texas.

During our working together I had acquired a quad. And this was because Paul had been an avid quad and trike rider from his youth. We both had trailers and Paul had one that could haul four quads at a time. He knew of allot of great areas in the region for off-roading and because of this whenever the opportunity presented itself him and me and some of our employees would take off for excursions in the woods. We didn't always obey the rules as far as where or when we could go somewhere with our quads. And although I am by no means justifying such behavior. I will say that we were never destructive in anyway. We loved the outdoors and respected it in every way.

On this particular weekend we were heading towards an area by Mt. Rainier. Our plan was to camp Friday and Saturday nights and we were going to leave on Sunday afternoon. We loaded up four quads on Paul's trailer and had our usual gear packed into the truck. Paul had a crew cab with a lid on the bed and everything we would need for the weekend was under that lid. We also had a number of 5 gallon military fuel cans lashed to the trailer. And so off we went. It was Friday afternoon. Paul brought us into yet another fairly secluded destination. Most of the places that we go into consist mainly of old logging trails or fire breaks.

Our habit is generally that of going into the woods a fair distance in order to insure that nobody else will spy us out. After setting up camp we pulled the quads off the trailer and went for a little exploratory stint. It's really nice forest over by Rainier. Somewhat dense in some spots and considerably more open in others. The perfect combination for a bit of rat racing through the trails and timber.

I guess we were gone for about 90 minutes or so when we returned to camp. It was getting late and we started a fire. We had cooked up some grub and had a few brews and at about 1 a.m. we hit the hay. In the morning Paul had been the first up and he was stoking the fire when I came out of the tent. As soon as he saw me he said this. Hey butch! Check this out. All of these longer pieces of wood were pulled out of the fire when I got up. They were all burnt up on one end and unburned on the other. I said to him that is really weird man are you sure?

He said of course I'm sure. Do you think I am hallucinating or something? I'm telling you that all of these sticks were just as you see them when I got up. I left them here so you guys could see them for yourselves. So are you saying that something was pulling sticks out of our fire while we were sleeping? Answer the question yourself Bro. What else could it be? The sticks didn't get out of there by themselves. By this time the others guys had climbed out of the sack and we were all standing around. All of us were in agreement that an animal would not want to get that close to a fire. And they certainly would not be willing to claw or bite the ends of burning smoking sticks and drag them around. This was getting weirder by the minute. We all thought that some pranksters must be in the woods with us. But who and where? And who would bother to traverse through the woods in the middle of the night to do such a thing? Why we could have shot them.

We ate breakfast and broke camp for a day of riding. We would typically ride for a while and then stop and take a break when we found an area worthy of a little exploration. Having returned after a day's riding that night was more or less a repeat of the previous night. We ate and drank and bullshitted until we were shot and then we crawled back into the tents. The following morning Paul was yet again the first one up. Only this time he dragged everyone out to see what had happened. We were standing around half asleep as he was jabbering about the sticks again.

Now I started thinking that he was getting up early and pulling the sticks out as a goof. Kind of like making up a ghost story just to freak everyone out a little. And if he was in fact doing this it was working rather well but I didn't say anything of the sort. We hashed it out amongst us pretty much as the day before and once again we took off for the day. Well that night we had a little too much to drink and Rich had nodded out sitting on a quad. I guess that one by one we had all gone into the tents and apparently whoever was last didn't bother to give Rich a shake to get off the quad and go to sleep. We were fairly toasted so nobody was really to blame. Well in the morning as we were crawling out of the tents and shaking off the cobwebs. I was the first to say to the others… where's Rich? Paul said the last time I remember seeing him he was asleep on that quad. We started shouting his name and walking around in the woods and no response was heard. This was not good. Where could he have gone? And why would he or anyone else for that matter have left the camp without saying something to someone? It just didn't make sense. We decided that we needed to get help and fast. So Paul took the truck and left us with the quads at the camp. He was going to get the police. While he was gone we kept looking but we didn't venture too far from the camp not wanting to compound the problem when Paul returned by him having to look for us as well.

About 90 minutes later Paul returned with 3 cop cars following. As the morning turned to afternoon there were more police arriving and a chopper was in the air as well. As you would imagine they questioned us rigorously. At first as a group and then individually. We were now suspects having done nothing. At some point two SUVs arrived with canines. They took a piece of his clothing and his sleeping bag and let the dogs scent them. And then they were off searching in the woods. We were helping in the effort by walking around and looking for anything that might give us a clue of his whereabouts. Everyone was calling out his name and one of the cops was using a megaphone belting out his name everywhere. At this point I was wondering if he had succumbed to some type of medical condition that caused him to lose his capability to think rationally. Perhaps he had just wandered away. I mean what else were we to think? I knew Alzheimer's patients to do such things. This was turning into a full blown search and rescue effort. They said the chopper had infrared and that if he was lying anywhere it would pick him up for sure. Several hours later we heard that one of the canines had picked up a black riding glove. We didn't see it or should I say we weren't shown it. We were just told that a glove had been found. One of the officers asked if he had his gloves on when he was asleep on the quad and we all agreed that he did. They were lightweight black calfskin gloves worn more for comfort and grip on the hand controls than for protection.

The search actually continued for a couple of days. Close to a hundred people were involved broken up into various search parties. Nothing more was seen or found on the ground or in the air. He had simply vanished. Now I won't bore you with everything that transpired over the next weeks and months. It was simply more questioning and more suspicion about us and our relationships with each other. It was the following spring when our softball league was starting up that some light was to be shed on what had happened. There were quite a few men's teams from the area who played each other from time to time during league play. The team we were playing that day was comprised of local law enforcement guys. I immediately recognized one of them as having been there that day in the woods. So I walked over to talk to him. He as well recognized me and after some small talk I asked if anything thing else ever came of the search besides the glove. He then said to me this is confidential my friend and I will deny even speaking to you. Get It? And I agreed. It wasn't just the glove that was found he said to me. And I said what do you mean? He said that the glove still had two fingers in it that had been torn off from the hand. Not cut but torn. I said to him there were no bite marks? And he said no. It was as though something had torn the glove from the hand pulling two fingers off in the process.

I said to him what the hell can tear the fingers off a man like that? He looked around to make sure nobody was listening and he said to me. The word is that they think one of the Big Boys got him. And I asked him what the hell a Big Boy is? He made some gestures with his body after which I said are you talking about a Bigfoot? And he nodded his head in agreement. There was no funeral ever held because there was no proof of death. Nor was there a body found. To this day he is just another missing person in the woods of Washington. And that my friend is my story sad but true. So there you have it my dear reader. For those of you who like to think of the Hairy Man as being big and cuddly. Such may not be the case. Do be careful out there in the woods. Be very, very careful.

The Overmountain Victory Trail Encounter

The following is a brief and yet interesting encounter story which was brought to my attention by Steven Casale who is a resident of North Carolina living in the Raleigh Durham area. This is his account in his own words. My friend Lance and I are avid United States history buffs. Anything related to our country and its history is on our radar screen and in particular military history. So we had made it our business that we were going to tap into walking some sections of the Overmountain Victory Trail.

Now it is not my intent to give you some grandiose history lesson. But knowing that most are unfamiliar with the trail I will give you a very brief introduction to it and the origins of its name. The trail actually runs from Virginia southward into South Carolina. It is actually quite long and arduous if you were to attempt the traversing the whole thing which is exactly what some early American defenders of liberty and freedom did. We owe allot to such individuals. I dare to say most pudgy Americans today couldn't even attempt it. In 1780 a British colonel named Patrick Ferguson in the month of September I believe. Had sent a military messenger to a group known as The Backwater Men who were located in the region of Tennessee and the western part of North Carolina. This by the way was in the heat of the American Revolutionary conflict. His message was a simple one.

They must cease in their opposition to the British Army and lay down their arms immediately. If they refused to do so he said the following. I will march with my army over the mountains and hang your leadership and I will lay your country to waste with fire and the sword. Well the month following Ferguson was dead. Killed at Kings Mountain South Carolina by the very Backwater Men which he had threatened the month before. Ferguson never got a chance to march through the mountains after them. For before he could do so they had already marched south through the very same mountains engaging him and his men and killing Ferguson in the process. So much for Ferguson. So we had marked our calendar to hike certain sections of this trail.

Now let me break for a moment to tell you something. These Backwater boys were tough and this trail is by no means a walk in the park. And they weren't wearing Bean hiking boots and down jackets. These were rugged no bullshit men. The kind of stuff this country was built on.

And just as a little side note. I read the other day that some railroad up north had announced that it will no longer be addressing its riders as ladies and gentlemen. Apparently according to them it's too insensitive to those who don't recognize themselves as being a man or a woman. So they are going to refer to them as riders or customers. I wonder what the Backwater Men would do with a man who likes to wear women's underwear.

It's just a thought. Besides the trail itself being beautiful in every aspect. There are also allot of artifacts and structures that are still intact in various locations to be seen along the route. It was along part of the old trail in Altapass North Carolina. Which was the location of a mountain pass through the Blue Ridge Mountains used during colonial times. That we found ourselves passing through a mature old apple orchard. An orchard that had its apples ripened in all of their glorious splendor upon our arrival. I apologize to the owners in advance but yes we did eat a couple.

And it was while we were sitting for a few minutes munching on some apples that we noticed something dark moving maybe 150 or 200 feet away from us in the orchard. We could only see flashes of whatever it was because of all of the trees between it and us. My immediate thought was that we were looking at a black bear. But that was to change quickly. Because just a few moments later we both knew that we were seeing the lower legs of something. And not only were they black and covered in fur but they were exceptionally large in girth. And then we could see at one point that whatever we were looking at was actually standing on one foot and extending its other leg backwards for balance. When it did this we saw the soles of the feet which in appearance looked like the bottom of a deerskin moccasin surrounded with black fur trim.

And the foot that we were looking at was not that of a black bear. It was a plus size. I mean really big. Even at that distance it looked like a snow shoe. And black bears generally don't walk on their hind legs and balance on one of them either. This thing really had our attention now. It was then that the legs which we had been focusing on left our view.

We were waiting quietly and patiently when suddenly this thing came back into our view walking on two legs between a couple of trees. For a brief moment we could see that it was a Bigfoot. A monstrous Bigfoot picking and eating apples in a daylight orchard. I actually started to tremble and my heart was racing a mile a minute. It didn't see us but we sure did see it. It was totally preoccupied with the feast at hand. I would say that a good estimate of the orchards tree heights would be ten feet or so. Some smaller and some considerably taller. The creature must have been 9 or 10 feet tall and massive in its proportions.

With one of its arms extended and a slight lean of its torso it was able to reach to the center of a fairly large tree. I am talking about 6 or 7 feet of arm length. And with the leaning making it 9 or 10 feet of total reach. At one point it must have knocked down or dropped something that it wanted. Because it kind of grunted in a way that made me think of the word frustrated. It stayed in a small area of what appeared to be 6 or 8 trees for quite a while and then it was gone.

We waited but didn't see it anymore and we couldn't see where it had gone either. It was truly remarkable. Quite a while later we found out that this was a public orchard. And I couldn't help thinking about someone with a family running across this thing while picking apples. We were making no noise when we entered the orchard. The trees were planted in and surrounded by lush green grass growing in soft soil. Our entrance was as quiet as quiet could be. And so I asked Steve to elaborate on the creature if possible and here is what he said. I briefly caught a glimpse of the face as it turned from one branch to another.

It slightly resembled that of an old American Indian portrait. Its face being very weathered and wrinkly looking. But the skin was dark and the nose was very broad and flat to the face. I would say the face was fifty percent covered with fur as well. The base of its foot looked like a giant flat piece of leather. Kind of like the finish on a really well used leather basketball in the street. This thing had to be all of 1500 lbs. Its forearms looked like my thighs and I go about 235 lbs. I just can't understand how this thing walks around picking apples. Going to and fro wherever it comes from and people aren't seeing it. How does that happen? We weren't exactly in the middle of nowhere when we saw it. And during daylight hours on a beautiful afternoon to boot.

You can't make this up. I mean I wish I could embellish it and tell you that we were stranded in a mountain cabin in the snow. And this Abominable Bigfoot tried to trash the cabin and kill everyone but such was not the case. And so there you have it. Make sure you leave some apples for the Bigfoot.

✗

The Mars Hill Incident

This story came to me from Jeff Landis who was formerly a resident of Long Island N.Y. now living in Pennsylvania. It is from his own lips that this story will now move forward. In the seventies I was involved in the trucking business. In particular my mainstay was that of hauling potatoes. And the two areas from which I hauled potatoes were Long Island N. Y. and the state of Maine. It was in and through this work that I had developed many relationships with people in Maine.

Guys who I had befriended and kept in touch with long after my days as a potato trucker had ended. The fellas in Maine called themselves Maniacs and with good reason. They lived a fairly secluded life up there and had embraced many hobbies to keep themselves busy. If it involved shooting, hunting and anything snow related it was right up the Maniacs alley. And so as not to leave anything out. Four wheeling and Moto Cross bikes were also at the front of their entertainment menu. In other words these dudes were doing everything that you and I want to do but for the most part cannot. Simply because of where we choose to live and all of the dos and don'ts involved with living there. This is wild country with very few inhabitants and even fewer people in law enforcement to watch over you.

I was always game for whatever the boys had up their sleeve and they loved to show off their toys whenever I was hanging with them. Thirty years or so after I was done with trucking I was still going up to hunt with them and hang out. Now I don't recommend this to you or anybody else. But some of these boys were regularly hunting out of season. Whether it's right or wrong I will not judge them. Especially on this particular trip because this time around I was with them. I will give them this much. Everything that they killed was eaten. So this time we were going to bow hunt for some whitetail deer and I had brought along my old Barr Apache 38 lb. recurve bow. I will not even come close to divulging to you where or when we were hunting so don't ask. What I will say to you is this. One of the guy's families owned an enormous tract of land. I am talking hundreds of acres. And this tract abutted and area that was robust with cranberries. Cranberries being one of the main agricultural products in the state. And there are allot of animals who love to eat cranberries if you catch where I am going with this. Now the boys had a number of locations where they would regularly set up trail cameras to keep tabs on what was moving in and out.

So we hiked in to retrieve some of the data cards or whatever they are called. In order to see what was around for the taking. If you have never been in the woods in Maine. The forest is so dense in parts that you could be lost 20 feet from the road and not know the road was there. And many people do get lost there every year. So these guys knowing the areas very well actually knew where there were some clearings in the woods. Some of them were quite small but they were clearings none the less. So we made our way in taking the cards and resetting some of the cameras in a few of locations. We had reviewed the footage and they were not impressed with what they saw. There were allot of small females and some short antlered bucks coming and going. The next day we went back and retrieved the cards from the newer areas that we had set the day before. Upon review we saw not one but two really decent bucks coming into the clearings. One was a healthy 8 pointer and the other a 10. But in reviewing the film we noticed something odd. There was a dark shadow that went through the cameras field of view. Now since the cameras take still shots when triggered. And those being taken every so many seconds. The first shot totally obscured the lens. And the second shot looked like a large black blurry shot of an elbow and forearm. One of the guys said it could have been the hind leg of a large moose. What the heck did I know? It was a fuzzy image of something that appeared to be dark.

So here was the plan. Two of us were going to stake out one of the clearings and two would stake out the other. We actually flipped a coin for the 10 pointer. The next morning we were in the woods really early. David and I were siting with camo on and our backs were up against some really good foliage as a backdrop to our camo. I will try to describe the clearing as best as I can. Dave had told me that this was a cranberry and spruce bog. In the morning light there was a heavy mist draped over the forest and everything was soaking wet with dew. The clearing was oblong in shape being maybe 150 ft. by 300 ft. or so. The clearing was tightly bordered by pointy blue colored spruce trees which varied greatly in their heights. They had a really staggered misty look to them as they faded into the fog. The majority of the clearing was a reddish golden grass that was about two feet tall well soaked and slumped over. And interspersed within that grass were hundreds of baby spruce trees and other plants with very bright red leaves. If my memory is correct these were the cranberries. So we sat and sat and sat. Now my range with my bow with accuracy was probably 25 to 30 yards maximum. I had never shot at anything any further away. So something would have to come relatively close for me to draw and hit it.

That's the art of bow hunting. Quiet and at close range. About two hours had gone by and the mist was all but gone when a doe came into the clearing. She was about 50 yards away but we weren't here for a doe. We were looking for the 8 having lost the coin toss. A little while later there were a total of 3 doe eating in the clearing. Now we were in the grass that I spoke of earlier. It was wet and made virtually no noise with our movements. Suddenly off to my left the 8 point buck came out of the spruce trees. We didn't hear him coming but there he was. He was looking at the 3 doe and around the clearing and started to slowly wander around eating. I already was in position for a great shot at him. I just needed to get into a crouch so I could standup. I put my broad heads nock on the string and ever so slowly started to stand. I drew back on the bow and shot. It was a great shot at a quarter angle right into the organs. I couldn't believe it. The buck lurched and jumped running into the woods.

Dave gave me a high five and said what a great shot brother! And it was a great shot. There was an immediate blood trail so it shouldn't have taken long to find him. That is to say for Dave to find him. If it was just me I never would find him. We got to a point where Dave said that the blood trail stopped and he couldn't find anymore. It seemed he said that the deer had fallen in this one spot and yet it wasn't there. In other words it died fell on the ground and disappeared. Even I could see that the area was flattened where presumably the body had been. For 3 hours we looked and couldn't find the buck. Dave said this was the first time that this had ever happened to him.

We made our way out totally at a loss for words. Especially after such a perfect shot on a great buck. And good hunters never want to leave a shot animal in the woods for this is taboo. The others guys couldn't believe what had happened to us and they had no luck with the 10 pointer either. The next day Dave and I were going to go where the 10 should have been and the other guys were at another location entirely. By the way all of these places were maybe within a 2 or 3 mile radius of each other. It was morning and we made our way once again into this other clearing very early. The conditions were as the day before being misty and foggy with dew everywhere. The woods kind of repeats itself here. There are very few plant varieties and those that are there are abundant wherever you go. This field was slightly smaller in dimensions. Dave and I were sitting about 75 feet apart from each other but we could see each other plainly in our camo. Virtually the same scenario played itself out for us yet again. A couple of doe gradually entered the clearing in the same way they had done the previous day in the other field. And then almost like clockwork there came the 10 pointer out of the woods.

He was about 150 feet away from Dave and over 200 feet away from me. He gradually lumbered around the clearing and over a period of about 20 minutes he was making his way towards my spot with his movements. Finally he was positioned about 35 yards from me with his head down facing me. I admit to you that I was a little bit antsy. But I put the arrow on the string and stood to my feet with the draw. A doe jumped and the buck raised his head and started to turn. I let the arrow go as it was turning and beginning to jump which admittedly was not a good move on my part.

A professional would have waited longer or passed on the shot altogether. But I was and am not a pro. It wasn't a terrible shot but I think I hit the shoulder bone. I could see that the arrow did not sink into the body upon impact and the buck took off. Dave said to me did you get him? And I told him that I thought I hit bone. If that was in fact what happened we would be tracking a wounded animal that might not even fall for possibly hours if not days. Never the less we began the track. Dave was looking for blood and there was very little. There were a number of narrow game trails through the woods that we were surveying. Trying as best as we could to determine which way this critter went. Back and forth we went for over an hour and the situation was not looking good for finding the buck. And then Dave shouted out Holy cow! What the hell is this mess? We had come upon a spot in the trail that was soaked in blood.

Everything around this one area was trampled down and in the middle so to speak was half of a deer's leg. I couldn't tell if it was the front or the back. Then Dave said to me I don't understand what happened here this is all very fresh. This just happened. The blood is still warm to the touch. Could this have been the buck you hit? What the hell happened here? We stood there looking around in somewhat of a state of shock. Dave began telling me about some stories he had heard through the years. Stories from other hunters saying that their kill was taken before they could retrieve it themselves. But taken by what? As we stood there Dave said look at this! He walked over and reached down picking up a piece of antler. Bears don't snap legs off and break antlers. And they sure as heck don't run away with a deer in their mouth. Let's get the hell out of here this is giving me the creeps. Later on we met up with the other guys who by the way had scored a nice buck for themselves. One of the guys had said that he once found a semi eaten doe that was maybe a day old lying in the woods that had one of its legs ripped off. None of them had mentioned the name Bigfoot that day but the thought had entered my mind years later.

When I had heard of animals being rendered disabled by Bigfoot on the hunt. We had seen nothing and yet we had seen everything if you get where I am coming from?

The Loggers Tale

This story is very brief and yet quite telling. It was brought to my ears by Jimmy Schmidt who many years ago was a logger in Northern California. Without any further ado here is Jimmy's story. In the late eighties I was a faller for a logging firm in Northern California. We were the guys who went into a sale ahead of all the heavy equipment. Our job was to take all of the trees down and ready the sale for haulage. Usually we went into a sale as a group of 4 to 6 men depending on just how big the workload was.

We also found ourselves frequently in some very desolate areas of timber simply because of the nature of our trade. I am talking about real no man's land. On this particular job I and 3 other guys took the crummy into the far end of the sale. This was some really thick and tall wood. The kind of place where men like us could get hurt if we weren't being careful. We were what are called Gyppos which means a contract logger in the trade. Having been contracted by a paper company to clear this particular sale and haul it to the mill. As we were working our way through the sale. Late in the afternoon I started to get wind of what I can only describe as a real stench. Not knowing what it was or where it was emanating from I kept working.

A short time later the punk on our crew came over by me and asked me what the stink was and I told him I didn't know. By the end of the day's work we had made it through about half of the sale and split. In the morning we piled into the crummy again with our gear and headed back into the sale for the second days' work. The stench from the day before was still wafting around in the air which I thought was very unusual having never smelled anything like it before. A couple of hours into the day the punk had stepped away to take care of business when he started shouting… Hey you guys come over here! Check this shit out!

So we all went over to see just what the commotion was about and there it was. A big pile of shit. It must have been 10 lbs. of crap and it was fresh. It looked human but the pieces were really long and wide. Some appeared to be 14 to 18 inches long and maybe 3 inches thick. There were no humans in here with us who could back one out that large I can assure you. And this was no animal turd either. We stood there stupefied looking at a pile of shit and wondering just what was in here with us. It was later that afternoon as we were tearing through the timber with the saws screaming when I felt like I was being watched. That's all I can say. A few minutes later I caught something out of the corner of my eye. And turning my head to look I saw a monster of mammoth proportions peering out from behind a large pine.

I knew immediately it was a Sasquatch. It was every bit of 12 feet tall and as wide as an outhouse. It stood there swaying back and forth apparently unafraid of the saws noise. I ran to the other men and pointed in its direction. It had already started to move off from where I had seen it but we were all looking directly at it unobstructed. As it was walking away it was looking back at us over its shoulder. Its butt must have been 4 feet wide and its legs and back were just as massive. The lat muscles in its back looked like 2 x 12s springing out of its body. And its arms were swinging slowly as it kind of bobbed away from us out of sight. To a man we all jumped into the crummy and took off. I quit the crew that day and never went back into the woods again. I never saw the other guys again who were with me that day either. And as a matter of fact I actually left some pay on the table uncollected. I asked Jimmy to give me any details about the creature he saw trying to be as specific as he could. Here is what he said. When it first came out from behind the tree. Really it didn't come out from behind it because it was three times as wide as the tree. It was just shielding itself from full view. Maybe it was moving and when I turned my body it had just stopped there to hide. At any rate when its face appeared it was looking straight at me. We were eye to eye.

The face did not look human. Yeah it had a nose and a mouth and eyes. But this thing was an animal not a man. The eyes were very dark if not black. The face and chest as well as the inner thighs had some exposed skin and the rest of it was covered entirely in dark almost black fur or hair. I remember its fingers for some reason. They looked like they were 10 inches long and I could see its teeth. It looked really angry but it made no sounds at all. Its two fang teeth looked slightly longer than the rest and I could easily distinguish them as being fangs. When I ran to the guys and pointed at the beast its back was now facing us and it had already covered quite a bit of ground as it was leaving the area. The back was completely covered in black fur and its head just swiveled on the shoulders. There was no neck whatsoever visible. Compared to the dimensions of the body the head looked somewhat small in size and was actually kind of sunken down in front of the upper back muscles. So from the back you could not see the head as I had from the frontal view. Everything about it was muscle bound and totally beyond the realm of human normalcy. The thighs alone must have been several feet in circumference. And its back was V shaped in a way that looked like it could bench press a ton. The creature's arms must have hung 7 feet from the shoulder and it was so gigantic that to me there would be no defense against it. I am not even sure a couple of well-placed rounds would be enough to take it down.

✗

The 1939 Cheyenne Mountain Sighting

This account was told to Joe Redmond by his Grandfather during a conversation in 1981. This is the story as it was presented to me by Joe. I think it was around 1980 or 1981 that my grandfather had come for a visit. We all were standing around in the kitchen helping to clean up after dinner. I think I was 21 or 22 at the time. Now Grandpa was quite the character. Always goofing around and trying to make light of things. But he was also quite sincere in word and in deed if you sat down with him for a conversation. Well it was sometime during the evening that the conversation turned towards the Roger Patterson and Bob Gimlin Bigfoot film.

I don't recall if there was a magazine lying on the coffee table or what exactly started it. But we began to talk about the film clip. Personally at that time in my life I thought that I had heard every story that Grandpa had to tell 10 times over. But this night was to be a memorable one. One for the records as they say. He broke into the conversation with a somewhat serious tone and said to us the following. You know Grandma and I saw some of these critters in the thirties back in Colorado. Well we were to a person stunned at what we had just heard. And I was the one who spoke up and asked him to tell us all about it. And as Grandpa was prone to do no story was too be a simple one. We were about to hear about the whole affair from scratch. By the way my Grandma had already gone on for her eternal reward at this time so it was just Grandpas account that we heard.

Grandpa wasn't rich but he wasn't poor either. He and my Grandma had moved to Colorado Springs for a reason. He was the sole representative regionally for a large mining supply company. And there was at that time plenty of mining going on in that entire region. So it was a matter of both convenience and necessity that they found themselves living there. He started to tell us that he and Grandma used to go and stay for the night at a place called the Cheyenne Lodge every couple of months. I guess it was a little retreat for him and Grandma. Who knows?

Now when Grandpa told a story you had best not laugh at him or disrespect him in anyway. He was all business and all truth when it came to his stories. He was a man's man. In fact he still had an antique Rheingold church key on his key ring in the eighties so we were all ears. He said that the round trip from Colorado Springs was 24 miles to the lodge and back. Incredible that he would remember such a thing. The Cheyenne Lodge he said was located at the top of Cheyenne Mountain and at the summit you were at 9,200 feet above sea level. The toll at the base of the mountain was a dollar and the trip to the summit was one of the most breathtaking rides and views that one could ever see. He bragged of his straight 8 Ford being up to the task every time. And then he began with the facts and figures as he was prone to do having a memory like a vice. He told us that the ascent was accomplished by a zig-zag course with an average grade of 7 ½ percent and no more than 10 percent. The road he said was a minimum of 20 feet wide and was flat covered with crushed granite for traction. He also mentioned that cars could actually pass each other anywhere on the road. Broadmoor, Colorado Springs and the Valley were constantly in view from the road as well.

He remembered with vivid detail many of the points along the road as you climbed. Hells Gate, Spiral Shelves, Paradise Trail, Cloudland Loop, Swing Sublime, Vista Grand Swing, Multi Vista Swing and Devils Horns. Each one offering some spectacular view or formation that was unforgettable. His recollection was that they had taken this trip some 15 or 20 times while living there. They also had one of the best zoos in America at that time alongside of the road at Swing 2 as he called it. When you reached the top the Cheyenne Lodge was there at the summit. He said it was like a small white castle with a rock wall and stairs leading you inside. I believe he said it was Southwest Indian style architecture. He and Grandma thought that it was the most unique and beautiful structure that they had ever seen and they loved this place. Inside there was a large and spacious lounge area in which there were many valuable Indian artifacts to see. There was an enclosed glass observation deck, lunch and dining rooms.

And a few guest rooms for those who wanted to stay overnight. He said that at that time for most people a buck was allot of money to pay for the toll. And many people did not even have a car suitable to safely make the climb or the decent. Things weren't as they are today. And he told us that some people lost their brakes and their lives on the mountain. It was on one of their many trips to the lodge that they had a custom of stopping to take in the view by Vista Grand

Swing. This was their favorite observation point. He went on to say that you could see for a hundred miles. The rolling hills, trees and mountains always in view. On this particular day they stood looking at what he described as a hillside with many pines growing on it. And in between the pines there were a few open areas where the hillside or mountainside could be seen. He said that the ground was tan or sandy colored in contrast to the surrounding dark green pine trees. Beyond this hillside and much further in the distance other mountains and even snow covered peaks could be seen from there as well. And that is why they liked to stop there.

He went on to say that on many occasions he and my Grandmother had seen wildlife walking on the slopes and in particular on this slope with the trees on it. As fate would have it on this particular day while he and my Grandma stood watching. They saw what they called 2 large gorillas walking on two legs emerge from the trees on the hillside. He said it was not so far that they could not tell what they were looking at. He estimated the distance they watched them walk at being 800 yards or so before they walked into another group of trees and vanished from view.

There were very few people sticking around outside at that time because it was warm. And certainly he said that nobody would be walking in the mountains covered from head to toe in black. He also said that they were very tall and had long arms based on the way the arms swung when they were walking. My father asked why he had never heard this story before. He said that the one time he started talking about it many years ago he almost got into a scuffle with the man he was talking to for telling him he was full of you know what. And it was after that happening that my Grandma told him it would be better to keep it to yourself.

And so he did. Well that was quite the story coming from the 1930s. Mountain gorillas walking the hills of Colorado. Simply amazing!

✗

The Merced River Sighting

This is the story that was told to me by Mary Stein about her sighting while hiking the Merced River. Here is Mary's brief but telling tale of what she saw. If you've never been there this trail is one of my favorite places for a short hike. Located near Coulterville California I would say that it is a moderately difficult hike for someone with a good pair of legs. I must have hiked this trail 20 times or more but I'm not counting. As we were getting along the trail this time around. There is an area where the trail takes a bend into somewhat of a canyon.

It can be kind of sketchy hiking here at times. There's allot of rocks to walk and balance on. And one could easily turn an ankle or worse if you are not careful. The trail can also change from year to year or even season to season. And in particular after any storms have passed through the area. It's not uncommon to come across large trees that have fallen across the trail or even areas which have been completely washed out by torrential rains. It's challenging but quite unique and beautiful. And so after this bend or I should say a hard right turn you enter into this small canyon where the trail starts to ascend. It's in this area where things can get really precarious to say the least. As you are ascending you pass several watering holes and a couple of waterfalls or cascades.

There are spots on this portion of trail where one side is predominantly jagged rocks and unstable ground surfaces. While on the other side you are looking at a steep hillside that is dense with trees. On this day we were approaching the bend or right turn where you find yourself positioned just slightly above the river. The trail becomes extremely narrow at this junction but it's still passable. At least this day it was. You are kind of tucked down into a shallow canyon with hills rising up on your right and left-hand sides.

The river looking ahead of you disappears around the hill to your right but at this juncture we could clearly see ahead of us several hundred yards. There isn't much at this point obscuring your view. The hiking surface here is now comprised of flat and oddly shaped pieces of gray colored stone that are everywhere along both sides of the river. And as the slope ascends to your left there is all kinds of somewhat low scrubby looking brush covering most of it. Brush that is spotted with many patches of taller trees here and there. The slope itself being very steep and likely several hundred feet or so in elevation. The point that I am trying to make here is this. If you were to hop over the river and try to make this ascent. It would take you quite a while to do so accompanied with some very heavy breathing.

And it is to this point that I am heading right now. So we are hiking down this stretch coming up on the bend some 5 or 6 hundred feet ahead of us. When we notice something or someone hunched over in the river way up ahead. All we could tell at this distance was that it was dark in color and crouching down in the river. We stopped to watch for a couple of minutes when whatever or whoever it was kind of partially stood up and quickly crouched back down again. Whatever this was we had now seen with that simple movement that it had two legs. And from this distance it appeared to be way larger than a man. My partner had already said to me that nobody would be dressed in black out here. Especially with a black hood on their head. I was in total agreement. As we started moving forward again in the direction of whatever this was it jumped up quickly and kind of flailed around to face us. Seconds later it made a couple of steps out of the river and out of our view. It was now temporarily obscured from our view by some trees and brush.

No sooner had it disappeared then it reappeared out of the brush and started tearing it up the steep hillside that I just told you about. This hillside was probably a 30 degree incline that was somewhat rough and covered in all kinds of brush and loose rock. This creature made it up the entire hillside which was maybe several hundred feet using its arms, hands and feet in possibly 30 seconds. It stood up and took one leisurely step as it went over the top and was gone. It was during this brief and fast climb that we both knew we were looking at a Bigfoot. It was mesmerizing to watch and both of us were left speechless by the encounter. As the two of us walked down to where it had just been in the river. We could see some rocks flipped around that were clearly wet on both sides. So now we knew that the Bigfoot was turning rocks over apparently looking for something in the river. Who knows what? We then saw the spot where it had disappeared for a moment into the brush. And based on what we had initially seen of it followed by when we could not see it. According to what it had gone behind we estimated that it was about ceiling height or 8 feet tall. We were now standing at the base of the slope that it had just scaled. And looking up the side of the slope the stamina and strength of this creature must be incredible to say the least. I stood there and thought to myself what would it take for me to do the same thing. And my answer to self was about 15 minutes or more on a good day with a couple of wind and water breaks.

Its agility reminded me of the fireman's competition. When they race up to a tower throwing a long ladder up against it. Followed by them climbing the ladder as fast as they can to ring the bell. It was the fastest dash I had ever seen. Uphill and near vertical it had scampered nearly 300 hundred feet in 30 seconds. I then asked Mary to focus on any details of the creature that she could recall and here is what she had to say. Well first of all it's like I said before. It was very dark in color. I would have to say predominantly black or such a dark brown that it doesn't really matter.

When it turned quickly towards us we could see its face. But with no clarity that I could accurately describe any features or anything like that. When it was stepping out of the river it like a human had to quickly watch its footing on the uneven wet stones. So it couldn't just immediately leap out of our view. But when it started to bust it up the side of the hill it was unreal. Its arms were extending and retracting as fast as its legs were pumping. It was very much like watching an old movie when they speed it up for laughs. It was virtually a blur of movements from bottom to top. But if I could freeze its movements visually at any given moment. That is to say when one arm and one leg was extended during the climb. It may have been 12 feet or so from hand to foot. It didn't pause for a single split second. Dirt and rocks and pieces of brush were flying behind it and around it like a whirlwind. And when it had reached the top without as much as a single pause it took one solitary step and was gone. I still walk this trail today and I am hoping to see it again. I didn't feel threatened at all and the fact is that it ran away from us. It was plain to see that it didn't want anything to do with people. That's not to say I would like to run into it in a corner. This was a large, large creature. I don't think saying that it was a thousand pounds would be telling a lie. It was a life changing experience of that I can personally attest.

✗

The Prospectors Letter

A letter was brought to my attention by an elderly woman named Clara Potts. She said that it had been in her family for many a year. And that it had been penned by her great grandfather William O'Leary who had died a man of great means. William being one of the few who had actually struck it rich during the California gold rush. I have taken very few liberties in the transcription of this letter. And now may I present to you the letter for your perusal.

Being a man of good conscience and in the fear of the Lord God Almighty. I have taken the liberty to set right in pen and paper the events and happenings which lead to the demise of the Wild Man by my own hands in California on that July day. I had been in Sacramento for the second time. Taking care of some business and refreshing myself and my animals. It was after several weeks when I decided that a man could die here more easily then he could alone in the woods. Especially a man who is hunting for gold. So I packed my horse and mule and headed out once more. I had enough provisions for sixteen weeks or so without taking into account what I would kill and eat. My carbine and side arm were with me as well as a large blade that I had won in a game of stud.

On my previous trip after washing many a dead pan. I had come upon some color in the North Country. More color in my pan then I had ever seen. Being however at the time of the discovery running low on provisions. I came back to Sacramento to resupply before heading back up north in the hopes of locating the origins of what I had panned and staking a claim to it. It was a steady 11 day ride to where I had found color. And I had no idea how much further it would take to find the lode if it was to be found at all. The Lord was good to me and the weather was grand. I had two good animals that were strong and able for the journey at hand. It was on the eleventh day that I reached the tributary that had given up gold on the last venture. And I started panning to confirm my whereabouts. My first 6 pans yielded enough gold to pay a man 3 months wages. Having confirmed my find I spent the night content. The following morning I packed up my bedroll and headed north for a day's ride. It was here that I came upon a choke point in the waters flow where I stopped to make camp. Since 3 days outside of Sacramento I hadn't run across another living soul. In the following 19 days I panned enough gold here to live out the rest of my days on. I had handpicked some nuggets that were as big as my horse's teeth.

One evening as I sat on a hillside in the hope shooting some food which I did. I came back to camp and made up a little smoker out of some boughs and branches. And commenced to lay out the slabs for smoking draping them over the wood. Having stoked the fire through the night by morning my meat was prepared. I had in my saddle bags hard tack, flour and some grits. And now I had an ample supply of smoked meat as well. I was not going to get greedy knowing that in this country it's not enough to find gold. But one must also return alive to make good use of it. This country is littered with dead men's bones. Men who were murdered in cold blood at the hands of those who relieved them of their finds. The next night I slept well. My carbine always loaded and at the ready next to me. It was during the night that I was awakened by my horses snort and a whinny. After which I leapt to my feet with my gun. As I tried to get my bearings by the fires glow looking towards the animals. I thought I saw something run away into the woods. But having been half asleep and it being very dark I was uncertain so I calmed the animals and sat by the fire the rest of the night. I was uneasy. It wasn't until sunup when I was caring for the animals.

That reaching into my saddle bag I realized that something had taken a fair amount of my smoked meat during the night. So I wasn't imagining something fleeing the scene that night. I wasn't alone here. And I knew that in these parts a single rifle shot could be the death of me in an instant. So I determined to pack up and start heading back to stake my claim. Having secured my gear and mounted up I headed out. I was working my way back down through a small grouping of trees when I heard something running and the bushes rustling more than a few times to my right side.

So I withdrew my carbine from its scabbard and held it at the ready. It was perhaps 10 minutes after I had withdrawn my rifle that a hideous scream came bellowing out from within the trees. My horse bucked sending me and my rifle ass over tea kettle to the ground. During my fall a second scream had sounded. And from my rather precarious position lying on the ground I suddenly saw a wild man type of beast charging at me from some 100 hundred feet away. My rifle thankfully had fallen right next to me and I grabbed it. This beast was running at such a rate that is not humanly possible. And as it had maybe 30 feet until it would prevail upon me I squeezed the trigger. It stopped in its tracks with a monstrous shriek as I chambered another round and shot it yet again. And still it did not fall. It stood kind of groaning and staggering when I finished it off with the third salvo. The beast fell to the ground lifeless. I laid hold of a long branch and stepping close to the creature I poked it. Its chest was not moving and it was lying at my feet dead.

I took a few moments to compose myself and retrieve the animals who had bolted. Thankfully the mule being tethered to the horse they had not gone far away. When I returned I stood pondering the beast and the events as they had unfolded. I was at once thankful that it had not killed me while I slept. For surely seeing it and its immense proportions it could have easily dispatched me.

I then realized that I had drawn it into camp with the smoking of the meat. For it was the very same smell that had directed it right into my saddle bag which contained it. Perhaps it had thought that it would stop me from leaving and have its fill of the rest and more. The hairy man's height was some 7 feet or so. Its mouth was open wide as blood trickled down its jaw. The teeth being exposed were like that found in my mule's mouth. Yellowed and cracked with age. It must have been the weight of a large grizzly. Certainly over 1000 lbs. and perhaps even better. Its palms were blackened and grayish in color. Cracked and worn like an old pair of chaps. And its fingers were the length of a large cigar and fur covered virtually its entire body but not densely. It was more like that of a man's hair covering his head. Its smell was horrific like that of decaying meat. I could not believe what my eyes beheld. The beast's feet were at least 2 or 3 times in dimensions that of my own. And its hands made mine look like those of a raccoon in comparison. I said a prayer for the beast and began to dig a shallow grave. I had to lash a rope to both the beast and my mule to drag it into the grave and then I covered it over. I had always felt a certain guilt after having killed the creature. If it was a man I would have confessed to it and rightly so. Having killed him defending myself from an attack. But it wasn't a man. And it wasn't really an animal either.

So it was with a heavy heart and as a matter of personal confession to God and man that I felt the need to pen this testimony.

✗

The Manitoba Evidence

The following evidential account was brought to my attention by Ashley Leveque a resident of Manitoba. This is Ashley's testimony of what she and her girlfriend saw in the woods of Manitoba. I am somewhat of a freelance software engineer. People hire me as their firm's needs may necessitate for weeks, months and or years at a time depending on what the requirements of the work entails. Because of this somewhat makeshift lifestyle I am afforded a fair amount of free time which I generally make use of for exercise and adventure. Two of the things which I enjoy most are cross country skiing and hiking. Having said that I generally do not go far from home to do either of these.

My home is somewhat like a small chalet which is constructed on a plot of land abutting a protected wilderness. It slips my mind how much land I am talking about behind me. But it is enormous in its scope being millions of acres. So typically I hike and ski within the confines of this wilderness. You couldn't ask for a better location. In all the years I have been living here I have not so much as once run into another human being in these woods when I am in there.

It was the winter of 2008 when my best friend and I broke out the skis for some exercise. We never clock how far we go or where we go. This enormous amount of untouched land affords us a plethora of directions to choose and trails to follow. And when the snow is down the potential for pathways is virtually endless. Our custom is to generally go as far as we feel we can saving enough juice for the return trip home. I would say that typically we can travel between 15 and 20 miles in an outing. On this day we were fairly deep into our outbound ski when we came upon what I will call a debris field. We were skiing on pure virgin snow and the only thing visible if you were to carefully look were some small animal tracks here and there in the fresh fallen snow. We had just gotten about 10 inches during the overnight and the temperature was about 25 degrees Fahrenheit. We quickly realized that what we were looking at was the remnants or insides of a rotten trees interior. Upon first glance we could see that the rotten wood and chips were strewn out in a pattern maybe 8 feet wide. And they extended out and away from the tree some 20 feet or so. As we were taking this debris field in it was clear that this had just happened sometime between the early morning and the time we had arrived which was about 10 a.m.

This we knew because there wasn't as much as a flake of snow covering any of the debris. And the snow had ended perhaps 3 or 4 a.m. At the same time we were surveying all of this mess we could clearly see that the entire location in front of the tree was completely matted down. In other words something was in front of this decayed tree for some time digging into and tearing apart its interior. We also noticed immediately a straight line of fresh gigantic footprints similar to the shape of a humans. Coming to the tree as well as going away from it. Being now out of my skis I stood next to a print in order to size it up against my own. With my boot on the ground next to the footprint it was approximately 12 inches longer than mine making its length about 24 inches. And its width behind the toes was about twice mine which was maybe 10 inches or more. Including the night's snowfall and what had been there on the ground already. We are talking about maybe a foot of snow total. And the snow was completely compressed within the print down to the pine needles and beyond. There was no melt in the prints and very little snow had collapsed within them. This had happened very recently. And because there was absolutely no wind there was also no freshly blown snow contained within the prints either. They were as perfect as perfect could be.

The stride of the creature that had done this was incredible. We laid one of the skis in front of the toes on one print in-between it and another. My skis being about 7 feet long it came up short of the next print by almost 2 feet. Making the step of whatever this was almost 9 feet from toe to toe. You could see plainly that it had come to this area fairly straightaway. And it had left the area side by side of the way it had entered. Two completely pure sets of prints. One set coming directly to the tree and the other set of prints leading away from it. As we crouched down to examine the prints we could clearly see toes but they were slightly splayed out. In fact the large toe or great toe was somewhat angled inward unlike our own. It was so perfectly imprinted that it almost looked like it had been cast. Many of the prints still had the snow that was raised up between the individual toes.

We decided to put our skis back on and try to follow the return trail for a while. I would say that for a mile or so it paralleled the entry trail and then it started to veer easterly into the woods. This direction leads to some extremely heavily timbered forest. It must have been about 2 miles or so when we ran across another debris field. This one was nothing like the first. It appeared like whatever this thing was had approached another tree thinking it was more rotten that it actually was. Because we could see as it apparently had that the rot was somewhat superficial in nature. And as it had apparently dug in about an inch or two it had found that the tree was still fairly solid at its core. The trail then continued outbound into the forest. We couldn't go any further for there was no end in sight. And whatever this was that was walking with a 9 foot stride. We were not looking forward to greeting it in these woods. It was apparent to both of us that whatever this was had been walking through the timber sampling decayed trees. Now I had heard of Bigfoot and seen some footage. And I had also seen the supposed footprints of the Abominable Snowman in the Himalayas.

You know the ones in a straight line going across the mountain slope in the middle of nowhere. These prints were exactly like that. They were made in a nearly perfect straight line like a gymnast on a balance beam. Totally unhuman like in nature. And the compression of these feet into the snow and pine needles was unmistakable. Whatever this thing was had incredible bulk. Even me with my boots on jumping and stomping down into the snow. I couldn't even come close to the type of compression this thing had created just casually walking. It had to have weighed many hundreds of pounds to do this. This beast must have been casually sauntering around in the timber trying to scrounge up some food. It's as simple as that.

I am sure they have a number of things to survive on and maybe what's in the decayed trees is just another one of the many things it eats during its days. This however has in no way hindered my going into these woods. I haven't seen anything else since then and many winters have passed since this occurred. To this day I haven't seen another set of prints. And there is certainly no human coming from the direction that this thing had come and gone. And especially with 24 inch feet. The toes alone within the compressed print were more than likely 3 inches long and as fat as a piece of kielbasa.

✗

He Must Have Run Away

Henry Jackson had contacted me with an unusual story regarding his mother's dog. And the circumstances surrounding the dog's disappearance in western Pennsylvania. Here and now is Henrys story. I think it was 1991 in the fall of that year that the phone rang at about 10 p.m. at night. But before I get into what transpired that night after the call. I think that I should backtrack a little bit. Because being a believer that hind sight is 20/20 I think that what must have happened that rainy fall night actually had started many weeks earlier. My parents owned a house in a somewhat rural area of western Pennsylvania. It was my father's parents' house which we had taken over after my grandparents had both passed. This had been a fairly good sized dairy farm back in the day with 3 large out buildings and plenty of grass. The house had 9 fairly large rooms and had been built somewhat along the lines of a southern plantation home. It was originally on 175 acres. But that had been reduced to about 20 with the sale of the rest many years back.

There hadn't been any dairy farming going on here in many, many years. But it was a beautiful home with a wraparound porch which ran across the front of the house and partially down the two sides. My mother insisted on living alone there after my father had passed some 7 years earlier. Initially I had thought of my wife and I moving in with her. This as it turns out was an idea to which my wife was opposed. So in order to keep the peace my wife and I stayed where we were which was about 8 miles away. As I recall it must have been in the spring of that same year that my mother had started to make somewhat regular calls about a prowler or the like being around her house. I had run over there at all times of the day and night to check things out for her and was never able to find anything unusual. I think she realized that this was becoming a burden to me and started to call the local police instead. Speaking for myself I must have been over there 15 or 20 times in a period of several months. And this in response to her saying that someone had walked by the window or that she had heard someone walking on the porch.

On two occasions she had told the police that someone was trying the door knob. At some point I actually had spoken to the police about her and the events surrounding her home when one of the officers said that maybe she shouldn't be living alone there anymore. This was something that I was in total agreement with but my mother in spite of the happenings would have none of it. And the calls kept coming none the less. I think it was in August or so that I told my mom I was going to get her a dog. Now my mom was in her late seventies. She liked animals but didn't feel she could walk it properly or take care of it. So I suggested that we could have a trainer work with a dog so that she could let it out alone and then all she would have to do is open the door and let it back in again. After much prodding she agreed to my proposal. So we bought a beautiful German Shepard from a local breeder which was followed up by engaging the services of a dog trainer who had actually worked with the local police department. And so now my mom had a big dog. It was after this that the nature of the calls changed. Instead of her saying that she saw or heard something. The call would always be that the dog was going crazy barking facing a window. Or scratching at the door barking while trying to get out of the house and this went on for a couple of months. By the way I must tell you that prior to my father's passing no such happenings were ever mentioned there. Neither had anything gone on there while we were growing up.

It all began years after my father not being around anymore. So now she had a dog but I was still going over there to calm her down and do a walk around the property. I told her to let the dog out if she heard something and he would scare whatever it was off but she would have no part of it. She had named him Freddie and said that he might get hurt.

Well it was on one of these phone call nights that it was raining quite hard outside. And she said yet again that something was walking on the porch and that Freddie was going ballistic. When I arrived I walked up to the door as per the usual. Prior to doing my flashlight walk around I noticed muddy prints that were more like puddles going around the porch. They ran up and down the entire length of the porch but I couldn't tell what they were from. I went in the house and asked my mother if she or the dog had been outside. She said that she let Freddie out prior to sunset but that she had watched him go out and do his business and had called him right back into the house.

Now I didn't tell her what I had just seen. But this entire nuisance ordeal had just taken a turn for the worse. There really was something or someone on her deck that night while she was alone inside with the dog. How could I possibly leave her alone knowing that? I told her that she has to let Freddie out if this happens or she would have to move. I told her that we got this dog for her protection as well as company and she had to let him do his job. I also said to her that I and the police can't keep running over here at this rate. It was driving my wife to the brink. About a week had gone by and she hadn't called once. So I stopped by to see how she was doing. She told me I am not going to call and bother you anymore. Now I was really going nuts. I told her you have to call if you feel in danger. This entire situation was going from bad to worse. Between my wife and my mother and her calling or not calling I was beside myself. I insisted that the next time this happened she had to let the dog out. On my way back home I stopped by the police headquarters and told them what I had seen regarding the muddy prints on the deck. They said you have to get her out of there. It could be a bear that may break in at some point. I agreed but couldn't help thinking about her saying that something was walking by the window. Bears don't walk around on their hind feet on people's decks.

Well that very night the rain was coming down in sheets again and the wind was howling. There was a real heavy thunder storm coming through the area. The phone rang and I answered it. My mother had a scare and let Freddie out. She said that she heard him barking frantically and then heard him make a loud yelp outside. The barking stopped abruptly after the yelp. It was then that she heard what she thought was a large branch fall on the roof. So back in the car I went in the pouring rain and wind. I went inside and said where is Freddie? She said that after the barking stopped he never came back to the house and she was crying in fear. I went outside calling him over and over but he never came. I was soaking wet and couldn't see anything. I told her to come and spend the night with us. The next day the three of us came back to her house. My wife took my mother inside of the house while I stayed outside. I looked everywhere and found nothing until I had turned the side of the house walking into the backyard. It was then that I noticed some large depressions in the soft grass and ground that had water in them. There was about 6 of them in a line. It reminded me of Herman Munster walking on the golf course. I put my fingers in one and it was about 5 inches deep. These were massive footprints of some kind. And as I kept walking I could visibly see more shallow one's going out into the pasture so I followed them out for a bit. The rain by this time had all together stopped.

As I was walking back towards the house I was thinking about my mother saying a branch fell on the roof. It was then that I looked at the roof of the house which was 3 stories tall and had 2 gables. Lying in one of the roofs valleys was Freddie's body. I knew it immediately. From the side of the house you could not see where he was. But the angle coming back from the field was different. I didn't tell my mom or my wife. We brought my mother back to our house that day and I told my wife privately that I would explain later. I actually came back later with the policeman when I was alone. I showed him the dog and told them of what had happened during the night. We put a ladder to the house and I pulled him down. The dog was so heavy that I had to drag him to the roofs edge and let him fall the 35 feet to the ground. The policeman and I both witnessed that his head had been twisted around like wringing out a towel. I dug a grave behind the barn and we buried him. I should mention that the policeman took a couple of photos of the dog and the depressions in the ground. This was a turning point for my mom. She didn't know what I had found but we convinced her to stay with us and sell the house. As for the officer and myself. After showing him where the impressions in the ground were. And seeing the dog with his head and neck all twisted up.

The two of us were in a quandary. You can imagine the thoughts that were racing through our brains at that time. And here is the point that I will end with. I have been wrestling with this ever since that day. We all like to think that we know something. In other words we like to think that we have everything figured out so to speak. But when you stand there looking at a 125 lb. dog thrown up onto a 35 foot tall roof. With its neck twisted around and dead. And you see and feel with your own eyes and hands 20 inch long footprints that are several inches deep. The thought goes through one's mind. Do I really know anything at all?

X

The Deer Feeder Evidence

The following is an account which was brought to my attention by Hank Lassiter. Formerly a resident of Nassau County Long Island N.Y. Here is Hanks story. Having spent 30 years of my life working for one of the departments in the City of New York. My retirement came to fruition and my wife and I decided to make a drastic move. Our home had escalated in value from our 235,000 dollars purchase price to over 900,000 dollars. We decided it was time to move from our 1/8 acre congested community into the country. She and I on more than one occasion had seen some T.V. footage of some community gatherings and festivals in West Virginia.

And we had thought that this might be the place for us to settle down in retirement. The two of us travelled down to Appalachia to have a look see for ourselves. For the most part the people were very nice with the exception of the losers who are still hung up on that Yankee garbage and bigotry. Which I always found to be idiotic considering they all drive cars which were invented by Yankees. And they all use electricity that was invented by Yankees. But there are no complaints about that. And we had experienced more than our fair share of the like in different ways living in N.Y. It's a crying shame that even church going people cannot love their fellow man. Nevertheless we found some beautiful country down there and decided to pull the trigger on a move.

There was no way that we would get hurt making a purchase in that region. We actually settled on buying a beautiful older home sitting on 50 acres which included an apple orchard. The price was 145,000 dollars. We started to get real accustomed to this quiet style of living. It was drastic but we liked it all the same. We found a nice church and tried to wiggle our way into some community activities and events. Over a period of about 2 years we had established a couple of good friendships with the best being my neighbor Ted. Now Ted was a real country gentleman. And he knew that I was head over heels in love with seeing the wildlife around us. So he suggested that I should put up a deer feeder in order to bring the deer in on a regular basis. He said that the only drawback would be attracting the bears. But if we hung the feeder high enough it would solve that problem.

So Ted and I on one beautiful Saturday afternoon set about assembling my feeder. We had gone shopping for the parts that would be needed the previous week. Teds plan was to take a 30 gallon drum and make a type of chute on it for the food to come down into. We were then going to assemble a steel rod through the top of the drum to which we would attach some chain. This chain was then going to be attached to a boat trailer winch. The cable from which would extend upward to an overhead cable suspended between two trees.

We would then attach the winch to a board on a tree from which we could hoist the drum off the ground. Whew! I hope you got all of that. The whole idea of this was quite ingenious. It being that you could lower the drum to the ground to fill it. And raise it up just high enough where a bear couldn't get to it. But a deer standing on its hind legs apparently could. And so after several hours of work it was finished. Then Ted told me that if I really wanted to have a little fun I could buy 1 or 2 trail cameras. And by attaching them to trees in some key places I could then see what was coming to the feeder. And it would help me to dial in the proper height for the drum to be off the ground as well.

It all sounded great to me and I purchased 2 cameras the following week. It really was quite allot of fun. I was buying some bulk feed locally and keeping it in one of my barns. My wife and I would go out and retrieve the data cards from the cameras and head back into the house to review them. We had seen some black bears trying to get at the food but they were unable to reach it as a full grown deer could just as Ted had said. Even though these were still shots it was fun to look at them. This went on for a couple of years and then after a while it kind of lost its luster to us.

We always saw the same deer doing the same things. And so it was that there came a time when we were not retrieving the pictures on a regular basis. But we were still looking maybe every month or so. Now I should tell you that a small John Deere tractor came with the house which had a trailer and a grass mower to tow behind it. I used this to cut the grass around the orchard and to bring sacks of feed to the feeder. We had set the feeder up out on the edge of the orchard some 300 yards from the house. Ted said that you don't want to put it to close to the house in particular because of the bears.

It must have been about 3 years into our living there that I went out to retrieve the cameras cards to review them. They were loaded with pictures as was always the case. There was no shortage of animals and I was putting hundreds of pounds of food into the feeder on a monthly basis. This day as I sat down on my computer to do my usual review. Much to my surprise on my computer screen pops up 8 stills of a Bigfoot at my deer feeder. There was no mistaking it.

Even I coming from Nassau county N.Y. knew what a Bigfoot was and it was gigantic! I was thinking that the drum was about 14 feet off the ground at its top. I later measured it and it was 11. The drum was about 4 feet tall and maybe 2 feet wide and the Bigfoots head when standing was about 1 foot into the bottom of the drums side view. He was about 8 to 9 feet tall. You could see him reaching into the chute with his fingers and grabbing grain. And in other shots he had his hand to his mouth. I immediately called my wife to see what I had found. She suddenly had a look of fear on her face that words cannot describe. She said to me that she couldn't live here with that monster walking around. Oh my God she said. It could kill us! So I called Ted. A little while later Ted and his wife came over and after they had seen the footage Ted said rather calmly. Well, well, well my friends. It looks like you have a resident Booger. His wife in the meantime was trying to calm my wife down about this whole affair telling her that it won't hurt you and the like.

I said to him have you ever seen such a thing in your life? And he said that he hadn't but knew that many others had. We were beside ourselves. And then Ted said this. You know this Booger has probably been in your orchard for years eating the fruit in season. And you would have never known it or seen it. But now it's gotten accustomed to your feeder when the fruit is gone. So I said to him what do you think I should do? He said that if I were you actually I would leave well enough alone and keep putting the food out. It's obvious that the booger means you no harm he's just eating. After they left my wife and I had no small discussion about this whole Booger thing. And at least for the moment she was not a happy camper. During the following months knowing that this Bigfoot was there I did take note of some impressions by the feeder. Which I now knew were from the Bigfoot. But I never saw it at any other time other than when I looked at the cards. He was coming to the feeder now on a regular basis.

It was in November that my wife and I were taking a week to go up north to visit family and friends for Thanksgiving. The relatives were all in an uproar when we told them our Bigfoot story. It was quite the topic to breach among Long Islanders. It was sometime during our stay that the thought had entered my mind that I had forgotten to fill the feeder before we left for the week. I don't know why I had thought of that but I did and it actually was troubling me. Well as it is with all good things the week's festivities came to an end. We said our goodbyes and headed back south. Upon entering the house I said to my wife that I had to tend to something in the yard. She said to me that after that trip you're going to jump into doing yard work? I told her I would just be a little bit.

No sooner had I stepped out of the back door did I set my eyes upon the barn doors torn off the building. I am talking about the lock clasps and hinges being completely ripped off and the doors were flung open. With the doors open the space was well lit. It wasn't like I was looking into some dark creepy space or anything like that. As I looked around at first I couldn't see that anything at all was missing. So why would someone rip the doors off my barn?

It wasn't until a few moments later that I took notice of some feed on the ground and the fact that the pallet on which the feed sacks had been laid was empty. The four 100lb sacks that I had on the pallet were gone. I remember standing there thinking who would risk jail time for stealing grain? And since I was really coming outside to fill the feeder. Now I had nothing to fill it with. So I went back into the house and told my wife to come outside and check this out. She stood there saying oh my God! Someone ripped us off while we were away. The two of us started looking around for anything else that may be missing but we found nothing out of order. And there were many things that would be of value to a thief. The house was as we had left it as well. So we called the local police to report what had happened. When the officer arrived he was as mystified as we were about the whole thing. In fact he said that who would go through the trouble of ripping these locks apart to steal grain and leave all of this valuable stuff untouched? I mean someone could drive in here unseen with a pickup truck but why bother? After he wrote up his report and looked around a little while he left wishing us good luck. I told my wife I was going to run up to the feeder with the tractor and that I would be right back.

As I was approaching the feeder I couldn't believe my eyes. The entire elaborate setup of cables and chains was torn down out of the trees. The chute was torn from the side of the drum and everything was thrown all over the place like someone threw a tantrum. It was then that I realized it was all the work of the Bigfoot. I went back to the house and immediately called Ted. He came over pretty quickly for a southern gent which generally he wasn't prone to do. Typically a little bit with Ted could be several hours but he was at my door in 15 minutes. I showed him the barn damage and pointed out the missing grain sacks. The two of us then went up to the feeder site to have a look see. Ted said to me and without any hesitation. This was all done by that Booger. He had heard of people putting food out for deer and damage being done when they stopped. But deer aren't capable of such damage they just move on. This Booger had grown accustom to this snack. And when he found it empty he got real angry. Ted said that he would bet it came back several days before it did the damage. Its anger building with every passing day until he blew his cork. That's when he came down looking for the food. And finding it in your barn he ripped the doors off to get it.

We were in agreement that I should leave everything as it was. Leaving the feeder site trashed and the barn door broken and open for a month or two at the very least. With no further food available for the eating in the feeder. And the apples in the orchard being long gone. We were certain that if there was no food around the Booger would move on. And so through the winter months I left all as it was. I did pick up on some tracks here and there around the property for the first month or two but then no more. We never had another incident around the home and we still live there as of today. I still see a print here or there in the far end of the orchard seasonally but nothing near to the house. So this Bigfoot is still around.

⨯

The Fire Jumper

This account comes from Ronald Johnston being a two tour veteran of the Army Airborne in the Vietnam War. This is his story told in his own way. I was still serving my second tour in Nam when the whole deal was called off. All the boys that could come home did and unfortunately many a good man was left behind. As I try to recall the remainder of the seventies it seems to be all one big blur. I was shot both mentally and physically having left allot on the table in Nam. I was as lost a soul as lost can be.

I found myself drinking heavily and smoking allot of weed which went on unabated until probably 79. It was at that time that I made a move to Lake Tahoe. One day while I was in the barber shop waiting for a cut. I noticed lying on a chair a magazine that was opened to a page with a blazing fire pictured on it. So I picked it up and as I began reading the article it was dedicated to a group of fire jumpers. It was a pictorial of them and the work that they do fighting forest fires. I can tell you now that something had begun happening to me that day from the moment I grabbed the magazine. As I looked at the photos of them arm in arm with their faces covered in black soot. I had found my destiny and a new reason to live again.

I spent the next year researching and doing everything that I needed to do in order to become a fire jumper and finally that day came. The reality is that I was a shoe in. I had been on several hundred parachute jumps. I was still physically fit and had been bolstering that fitness over the year that I just mentioned. And on top of that I was certified as a field medic. I had been welcomed into a team in the Northwestern United States. Now if you know nothing about us or what we do. Basically we are air dropped in many severe fire situations into locations where the fire is believed to be heading based on the terrain, fuel supply and the direction of the prevailing winds. Our job is to create fire breaks so that when and if the fire should make it that far it will have nothing left to burn. In other words if we are lucky and have done everything that we can. The fire will reach a point where it will just burn itself out.

Once we are dropped in it can be a very lonely affair. We have to be cautious not only of ourselves. But we must be attentive at all times as to what the advancing fire is doing. In many situations the only help we can rely on is in fact ourselves and air support. And in some cases ground support if and when we reach suitable areas for them to come in. It was not unusual when we were in the heat of it all to see all kinds of wild life running about here and there. They know what's going on to a certain degree and are confused. Herds of wild horses or deer and everything else that you can imagine heading for cover trying to escape the flames and smoke. As it turns out this particular August about which I am speaking. It was believed that a lightning strike had started a blaze in northern California. There was already 5000 acres ablaze when we were called in. We began to work an adjacent hillside to where the burn was most intense. Felling trees and clearing underbrush. We had been working as a team for many hours clearing this break when the team leader made the decision that we should climb the hillside and work our way down near a canyon area to our west.

We had with us topographical maps of every location into which we were dropped. The thought being that if the fire had advanced in the direction of the canyon. It would either burn out by its edge or burn down into it making it easier to contain. Everything in this business is a gamble of what ifs. As we were coming over the side of the hill beginning our descent toward this canyon. We noticed from our vantage point a line of four creatures walking away from the canyon to the north. They were black in color and walking like men.

One of the guys who was actually a woman. Yes women are fire jumpers also. Had pulled out her binoculars and said they were Bigfoot. We couldn't believe it but after about 5 minutes we all new that they were in fact Bigfoot. All of us having had a chance to peer through the binoculars. There were three large ones and one smaller one obviously fleeing from the smoke and impending danger like all of the other creatures were. We had no time to continue watching but had plenty to talk about. When we had made our way down to the canyon we had begun our work forming a line as was always the case. I and Steve Mays were closest to the canyons stony outcroppings. We were now in the area that the Bigfoot had either been or at the very least walked through.

About two hours into the work Steve said to me. Hey Ron! What the hell is that? Oh my God it's a person! Or what's left of them anyway. We both laid our tools down and motioned for the team to come down to where we were. We stood there looking upon the skeletal remains of a human being with its clothes still on. It was wedged between two large boulders. As we stood there looking we all started realizing at about the same time that something was not right. The body had a collared shirt on but according to the way the boots were facing the shirt was on the skeleton backwards. And then on even closer inspection one of the men pointed out that the shoes were on the wrong feet. Which once he had directed us to the curvature of the boots we knew it was true as well. The skeleton I should also mention had no skull. And although we had not looked around much it certainly was not next to it. This skeleton seemed to have been there for quite some time. The clothes were already fairly weather-beaten. So much so that the bones were visible through the clothes in many areas. We thought to ourselves and to each other. Who the hell would walk around with their shirt on backwards and their shoes on the wrong feet? Especially out here in the middle of nowhere. There was no backpack or any type of gear whatsoever present with the corpse. Just the remains of a blue shirt. A pair of tan trousers and brown hiking boots.

There weren't even any socks or underwear visible. It was then that we started saying that if the clothes had been removed from the person at some point in time. Who or what wouldn't have known how to put them back on again in the right way? I mean if you are going to go through the trouble of dressing a dead man it's easier to put the clothes on correctly. We all agreed not to touch the remains too much. We did try to see if there was some type of I.D. which we couldn't find. It was quite a pickle that we found ourselves in. We all knew that whoever this person had been they didn't just lay down where we found them. Especially when the flesh was still on the body. This body must have been jammed into where we found it. And it didn't get dragged there either. Someone or something had pushed this body hard into this opening to hide it. We also knew that we weren't going to carry this skeleton out. Not now anyway and not without investigation. There was no help that was going to come into this area at this time to do anything with the body. In fact over the next couple of days the entire area may well be overrun with fire. We radioed our find to command and we continued to battle this fire for the next 10 days. At some point we met up with ground support and relayed where the body could be found.

About one week later I and two others from our group went back into the canyon with law enforcement. We brought them right back to where the body was and thankfully the area had been spared from the fire. This time we had come back in with a couple of stump jumpers. These are really beefy off road fire trucks. We were able to get fairly close leaving ourselves with only a short hike to the scene. The Sheriff's Department was now treating this as a full blown crime scene. When we started to bullshit with them about the clothes being on wrong. They said that this wasn't the first time they had seen this or heard about it. They said that through the years quite a few bodies have been found not only in California but around the country in this fashion. Some say that it may be the M.O. of some mad serial killer. After this day it was the last we heard about this body that we had found. Now I know that you are interested in what we saw as far as the Bigfoots go. First of all anybody who has a brain could tell we were not looking at large people walking away from a fire dressed in black. Secondly even at a great distance the walk and stature of what we were seeing was not human. There is a very wide spacing in their steps. And the upper body has a definitive forward lean which a person does not exhibit when looking at them from the side. And the third and most definitive aspect are the arms. I guess it's because of the weight and length of the arms which by the way were visibly very long. That they very deliberately and slowly swing forward and back when they walk. You could also see when they turned or twisted their upper body. That the arms would kind of flail outward. Like the action of that carnival ride that has the twirling swings hanging on chains. It is very distinct. Well my dear readers at this time I would like to offer special thanks to our brave fire fighters for all of the hard work that they do. May God bless you all and keep you free from harm.

✗

The Hobo Camps

Although it is not very lengthy and it comes without tangible evidence of any kind. This story was told to me with such intensity and what I believed to be truthfulness. That I felt it was worthy of inclusion in the book. Here is the story as it was conveyed to me by Charlie McGowan. In 1963 I was coming of age for the Nam draft. There was no question in my mind that I would be drafted it was only a matter of time. So I decided to dodge the draft and head for the west coast. Many in my family were saddened by my decision at the time. But I would not be swayed. The bottom line which we all know now and didn't believe then. Was that this fight was not about battling someone with desires of world domination. But rather it was a spitting match and a money maker for those who wouldn't have the guts to fight themselves. My thought being at the time that I left. Was that I could get lost in a crowd as well as anyone else. And the west coast was as far away as I could get in this country without leaving the country entirely. So I was willing to take a shot.

When I first hit the coast it wasn't long before I found myself hanging with the street hippies and flower children. People who were basically wandering aimlessly through life. And who were for the most part doped out of their minds day and night. This was the rebel anti-war crowd that was predominate in California at that time. Soon after I had arrived I found myself hooking up with a guy named Jimmy Byrnes. He like me was on the run. He had a dive room in a flop house and his philosophy was this. Work cheap and work for cash. This way people would be so happy to have you they wouldn't dare fink you out. And the second part of his philosophy was to keep moving and so we did. We were now a team. Thumbing rides was much too risky so we had adopted the practice of jumping rail cars from location to location. I had officially become a hobo.

It was an extremely dangerous racket. Sometimes we would check the doors on freight cars at night hoping to find one open that we could sneak into. Other times we would cling between two cars sometimes for hours at a time as the train ran down the tracks. Occasionally we would even make our way to the roof and hold on for dear life. And God help you if you had to go to the bathroom or got sick. There was always the threat of being seen and having the cops flag the train down but we were willing to take the risk. The tracks were littered in those days with many who fell to their death under the cars doing exactly what we were doing. We soon found out that there was a network of camps running up and down the state. Thousands of guys like us and others creating these God forsaken ghettos in the woods out of trash, scrap wood and sheet metal. It was hell and I was starting to wonder if I should give it up. I think it was in the second camp that we had hit. Where one night one of the drunks said to us be sure that you sleep close together. We looked at each other for a moment and I know that we both thought the same thing. What was this some kind of fag camp? But when I had questioned him about his motivation he told me bluntly. Guys disappear from this place at night. In particular when the vegetable season is over which is now. Well this dude staggered off and the two of us realized that you could lose your life in these woods for a 5 dollar bill and no one would ever know the difference. We stayed awake that entire night.

The next day I caught up with the same cat from the night before. Only now he was sober relatively speaking. I asked him about what he had said last night about guys disappearing. He looked me square in the eyes and said the hairy men take bums like us for food. I shook my head in disbelief. I said to him what the hell is a hairy man? And he told me there are things in these woods that man knows nothing about. And when the food runs out in the fields they come to us looking for a meal. This was the craziest thing that I had ever heard. Hairy men eating humans. This guy had to be touched in the brain was all that I could think. That afternoon we split yet again. There was no way we were going to hang here for another night. We slept in the woods by a freight yard for two days hoping to find an open car which we finally we did.

Being a hobo was allot like being an addict. If people dug who you were. Wherever you were they would take you in and hook you up with what you needed to know. You became part of the in crowd. Can you dig it man? And so on our next jump off we found another camp and got hooked into a little work as well. We worked at a masonry yard for several weeks. We were crashing out inside of some cesspool rings at night. The owner knew it but he didn't care. We were giving him a good day's work on the cheap and he knew that we were runners. He had a portable toilet in the yard and let us use his sink during the day. We were taking hose baths and washing our stuff outside in the yard. In keeping with our philosophy of always moving on we split this scene after about 12 days and went back to the camp.

When we got back a number of the guys said to watch our butts because one of the guys was taken in his sleep last week. And we said taken by what? They said that one of the big hairy suckers got him. It pulled him right out of his box screaming and kicking into the woods and he was gone. All of his crap is still right over there. Now no hobo would leave his stuff anywhere. And he had left a duffle bag full of clothes and a radio in the camp. That was the end for me. I hung in the camp for a few more hours while a couple of these guys were talking about a boneyard they had found a few miles north. A bone yard where there were human remains scattered around. An hour later I was on the highway thumbing a ride. I didn't care if I got caught or even arrested. I was done with this whole scene man. Hairy men eating people and bone yards. I was done.

It took me almost two months to get home stopping to work for some food and lodging along the way. When I got home my draft number hadn't even come up. Which it would eventually. And when it did I had a change of heart and went into service. Thankfully I had a good working knowledge of engines which parlayed me into a stateside gig. And I am obviously alive and here today to tell the tale.

✗

Highway Patrol

This account came to me from a retired law enforcement officer. He told me that he went through such ridicule over this encounter that I agreed not to even mention what state he had worked in. Here is John Sorenson's story. I was a 24 year veteran of the force when this encounter happened. The only thing that I am willing to say about where I was that night is that it was the northeastern United States. I was on highway patrol that night. Most of the old timers preferred the night shift because it was typically quieter than the day. On this particular night that I was on patrol the weather was crisp and clear.

Now there were a couple of stop signs that I would generally set up on early in the shift. And then I would hit the main highway with the radar gun later in the night. I had a spot that I would back into. It was a grassy edge of the highway with the forest at my back and a rock wall to my left. By the time a speeder made it around the granite outcropping and saw my squad car. The gun had already bagged their speed. I had already tagged a couple of speeders that night and was preparing for the next back at the same spot. I had turned the car off momentarily and stepped into the trees to take care of some business. It was a pitch black and moonless night. And trust me when I tell you there was no one around in this stretch of highway. Just woods and rocky walls. I was just finishing up and turning towards the car when I could see headlamps shining ahead of a car that was coming around the bend towards my position. Remember nobody could see me here until they had virtually passed in front of me.

Just as I had seen the glare of the oncoming lights the cars horn started sounding and they were leaning on it heavily. Well they flew by and kept going. I had taken maybe three steps toward the car when a large dark mass came into view from around the wall on my left. Whatever it was came walking along the shoulder. It was visibly huge and I grabbed for my service revolver. I was in the dark and out of my patrol car and some type of massive thing was walking towards my position from my left-hand side some 15 feet away from me. Immediately I knew this was what they were beeping the horn at. As I was reaching for my flashlight out of its belt loop I said hey you! Stop right where you are! And I hit it with the light. When I did so it had already turned toward me and growled. And its eyes were glowing red before the flashlight had even hit them. When the flashlights beam met its face it let out the loudest most intense roar that you could possibly imagine. Its head held high into the air and screaming like King Kong. The mouth was wide open and I could see its teeth.

I was about to pull the trigger when it snarled at me while turning towards the road. It took maybe four fast steps or leaps clearing all

4 lanes and both shoulders and it was gone into the woods on the other side of the highway. This entire episode had taken maybe 45 seconds if that. I jumped into the car starting it up and flipped on the headlights. I could see nothing. So I turned on my spotlight and moved across to the far shoulder. And when I did I caught it briefly looking in my direction with its red eyes beaming in the darkness. The damn things were like red reflectors on a kid's bike. It turned and high tailed it out of sight into the woods.

There were four units total on patrol that night. And back at the station house were the dispatcher and our sergeant. When I got on the radio I started to tell everyone what I had seen. Not thinking of being taken as some joker which is exactly what happened. The chatter was ridiculous coming over the speaker. And the dispatcher said to me that I should fill out a report when I got back. Aside from all of the bullshit that happened after the fact. This Bigfoot which I know emphatically that it was. Was all of 7 to 8 feet tall. When the light hit it I could see dark skin on its face with some fur like a beard. Its teeth were large white squares like big chicklets. The fur was quite long and matted. And its head and shoulders were like one unit. Kind of like a turret on a tank. The head looked like it was plugged into these massive upper shoulder muscles and the face was as mean looking as mean can be. It was the most frightening thing that you could imagine and then some. I don't know why I didn't pull the trigger. But when you fire a round as a cop it's a big deal. And firing a round at a Bigfoot… well you can just imagine.

As the thing turned to cross the street at the shoulders it must have been 5 feet across. The fur on its butt was totally encrusted with leaves and crap. And while it was near me the stench was sickening. Like rotten garbage or roadkill. The next day I came back to the spot with my truck. Parking on the shoulder I walked back to where it had come from. I could clearly see heavy impressions in the soft grass of the shoulder. And when I went to the other side where it had run from view there were more even deeper impressions in the down slope of the grade. These prints were large and maybe close to 20 inches long. You can't believe the crap that I had to put up with after that night. And it wasn't because of the event completely. But I retired shortly thereafter having served my time with 25 years of service. There you have it my friends. Yet again another sighting by another policeman.

The Helenbar Lookout Trail Sighting

This sighting was brought to my attention from a couple who reside in Toronto Ontario Canada. This is the account as given to me from Robert and Grace Kuntz. My wife and I are both somewhat amateur naturalists. Our home is filled with books and artifacts from years spent hiking in the woods. We have pressed leaf and fern collections. Castings from wolves and other animal tracks. And all kinds of oddities from our many excursions throughout the years.

We have handmade lamps from tree limbs gathered in the forest. And some of our furnishings were handcrafted by artisans from the forests to our north. I only mention this so that you can kind of get a feel for the type of people we are. At the time of this sighting our two children were 9 and 12 years old. Sofia being the oldest and Eddie the younger of the two. At least twice a year we would go camping. But many other days we spent together hiking and scavenging in a variety of locations. One of our favorite locations is the Helenbar Lookout Trail in Mississagi Provincial Park. It's not too far from Toronto and it is an absolutely exceptional place to hike and camp. We had probably been there a dozen times or more before.

The campground is named Semiwhite because it is located adjacent to Semiwhite Lake. The trail takes a few hours in and of itself to traverse. So we generally bring a picnic type lunch along for the midway point. A break which we typically take in an area known as the Second Lookout at which point you are close to yet another lake named Helenbar. There are many animals in this region including deer, moose and wolves. And it is not uncommon to see wolf tracks on the very hiking trail that we walk on because this same trail is used by them at times. In fact this is where we had taken the casts which we have at home. Many people are afraid of wolves but this is an unfounded fear. They are actually quite shy and have extremely keen senses of both smell and sight. The only indication of the wolves' presence known by a human will typically be their howling. Which we have heard on many occasions. We had decided this time around to go in September. October and September being the rut season for the moose. We were hoping to stay out of harm's way and actually see a moose on this outing which is easier said than done. In fact as large as they are it is extremely rare to see one here.

As we began our hike this September day and as I begin to tell you about it. I will do my best to kind of give you a good idea of what we were seeing and what you would see if you were there with us. The trail is kind of a big oblong loop. It heads out towards Helenbar Lake and then swings back around with the return leg running along the shore of Semiwhite Lake. These are two entirely different bodies of water. Helenbar being very shallow and Semiwhite being much deeper. In fact Semiwhite is home to lake trout, whitefish and allot of minnows. Most of which like the deeper water. While Helenbar Lake on the other hand at its deepest point is less than 15 feet. But it supports a robust population of brook trout. As you enter the trail you get a real sense that you are leaving the world as you know it. It's like entering Middle Earth or some fantasy forest. The moose by the way live within this place because everything that they need throughout the year can be found right here. And the wolves of course are here because of the moose and the deer. It is the perfect ecosystem at work in every way. One also needs to exercise great care at his time because the moose can be a little bit edgy during the rut.

As you begin you are going uphill and there are many boulders which were left here by the glaciers. They are referred to as conglomerate rock also known as glacial erratic's. One of these rocks which was left here by the glaciers. Which more than likely had been dragged hundreds of miles is of immense size and proportions. There are also quite allot of ferns growing on this huge boulder. As you continue along the route you will see a large swath cut through the forest. This is done intentionally by the Province of Ontario. The young growth which springs up in these areas provides reachable and edible food for the deer population. Passing the boulder field you start to enter into the heart of an upland forest.

An area filled with red oak, yellow birch and sugar maples. All of these trees are actually at the extreme northern limits of where they can grow and thrive. And directly alongside of them you begin to see what is known as the northern boreal forest. A place where spruce and balsam firs now takeover. You are actually walking at the very cusp of a transition zone between two different forests. You will also begin to see here as you continue your hike many stumps which are remnants of the logging for white pine which occurred here years ago. Occasionally there is also a large root ball visible from a tree which had fallen throughout the years. There are also many clusters of Lady Fern visible in some of the more moist and shady areas of the forest.

As you approach what is known as the First Lookout there are very steep rocky faces which confront you. These stand in stark contrast to the surrounding beautiful forests. And from here as well as the Second Lookout you can see the shallow and lovely Lake Helenbar. In this area between the two lookouts there are actually many large trees which have been uprooted by the wind leaving their enormous root balls exposed. On this day we had begun our descent from the Second Lookout and had probably walked maybe a quarter of a mile passing many of these fallen trees. It was then that up ahead a large male bull moose emerged from the forest coming from the shore area of Lake Semiwhite. This is one of their favorite feeding zones. They love the aquatic plants like lilies which grow in the shallows at the lakes edges. He was right in our path and making his mating calls as he lumbered along.

We didn't want to get to close so we started to backtrack. As we did so we were snapping some pictures and trying to enjoy the moment and the sighting as much as we could while still being very cautious. He really seemed as though he was not going to move on any time soon so we decided to back up near the area of the fallen trees and hang out for a while. Our only other alternative being to hike completely back the way we had come. As we were waiting Sofia said to me. Hey Dad! I just saw something come out from behind that big dead tree back in there. Now there were quite a few dead trees so I asked her which one? She was pointing at a large root ball maybe 150 feet away from our position.

As we all stood there focusing on this giant root ball. My eyes were drawn to what I perceived as being a large black furry arm which was wrapped through and around some of the old roots extending from the side of this ball. And no sooner had I begun focusing on it when a large black head jutted out from behind the ball looking right at us. My daughter and wife said almost simultaneously. Oh my God…Look at that! It was the head of a large black creature that was hiding behind the ball. As we were looking at it the head started twitching back and forth in a crazy manner. I mean it was going left and right really fast. And the arm which by now I knew was an arm had been pulled back out of view. My daughter said I'm scared. And the two children came really close to us. I reached down and grabbed a large piece of branch and broke it off into somewhat of a club. And as I did so this thing took off at a frantic pace running through the trees. It moved so quickly that it was almost a blur. We could hear it crashing and thrashing through the trees as it ran. We were absolutely in shock and my daughter was in tears with fright. We started to walk back to where the moose had been looking over our shoulders the entire time. And thankfully when we reached that area again the bull had moved on. About 45 minutes later we were back at camp and safe. As far as what this creature looked like. We actually for a brief amount of time had a reasonably good look at it.

When I realized that I was looking at an arm after its head came into view. I would estimate that just its arm alone had to have been 5 or more feet in length. I say this because I had to have been looking at well beyond 4 feet or so slightly above what was its elbow. This arm was heavily covered in what seemed to be thick blackish brown fur. When its head moved into view we could see a portion of its body through the root ball of the downed tree. It was then that we knew it had a body and it was standing upright. It looked like a big gorilla. But of course we all know that there are no gorillas present here or anywhere else in the states. And even if one somehow fell to earth here it would never survive the climate. This was a Bigfoot. The head had somewhat longer hair on it. And when it started flipping its head left and right like it was going crazy. We could see the long hair flipping back and forth. It looked like some lead guitarist in the middle of some mad jam session.

It was doing this twitching motion so fast that it was hard to comprehend why it would do so but it was. Then it quickly moved away from the roots and began running into the woods. And it was doing so leading with its arms and hands. Just like plowing everything out of its way. It was like a whirlwind of activity parting the brush as it pushed forward through the undergrowth. It was basically slapping saplings and brush aside with seemingly no regard for getting hurt. Seeing it was very bizarre indeed. We could clearly see when it moved from the cover of the roots that everything about its body was extra-large. The biceps and forearms looked like tree limbs. Its upper thighs from front to back must have been 16 inches deep and its butt cheeks stuck out well beyond the thickness of its thighs. Completely different than a humans buttock appears.

It was very tall well-formed and muscular. I would also estimate the shoulders at 4 to 5 feet in width because I saw it at virtually a quarter angle before it disappeared in the woods. You have to understand that the undergrowth is so thick in some of these areas. That all you had to do was step into it 10 feet if you could and you would vanish from sight. At no time did it show its teeth. But as most people already know or have heard its hands and feet were extremely long. And I did notice when the feet were lifted as it stepped that the bottoms looked like a flat leather shoes sole with fur coming down the edges. We could faintly hear it thrashing away for a fair amount of time and then it was silent. Of course we don't know if it had broken into a clearing or if it was just too far away at that point but the encounter was over.

✗

The Rutland County Sighting

This account came to me by way of Danny Sheehan. Who is by the way unrelated to me. Let's hear what Danny has to tell us about his encounter. My Uncle Jack who in retirement had moved to Rutland County in Vermont. Had been employed as a graphic artist for most of his life. He also more than dabbled in watercolor painting as a hobby for an equally long period of time and was very good at it. And being a city boy for most of his life he would head to the country whenever possible in search of some solid subject matter to paint. His favorite themes being fly fisherman, covered bridges, old farmhouses and boats. He also had totally taken to fly fishing which gave birth to the painting of others doing so. I would go to visit periodically in order to fly fish with him.

Within the surroundings of his area alone there was a tremendous offering of many great places to fish for brook trout. It was a veritable potpourri of fly fishing pleasure. We were heading this day to a place where we had been several times in the past. It was my uncles favorite spot and with good reason. Not only was the fishing superb but the location was some of the most beautiful Vermont property that you will ever set eyes on.

It was here several years ago while I stood on the rocky bank of the creek fishing. That he was on the other side of the creek facing me with an easel using me as a model for a painting. A painting that I have in my home to this very day. We were near a town called Wallingford and we were fishing a body of water known as Otter Creek. He knew a gentlemen who owned an old farmstead that this particular creek passed right through. It was the combination of the man's property and outbuildings in conjunction with the shape and natural design of the creek in this area which made it such an outstanding location. I will do my best to bring you into this picture.

The farms original owners were cheesemakers. Creators of what we now know and enjoy as being Vermont cheddar. I would say that the acreage was about 40 give or take a few. There was a large farmhouse built in the middle of the land and two very large unpainted and well weathered barns could be seen as well. Standing at the properties highest elevation which was where the house was built. When you looked out over the farm it was mostly cleared with the exception of some large trees being left for shade and or esthetics I would guess. The land was rolling and terraced being completely covered in grass. And there were a number of large sections which had been enclosed with split rail fences and gates.

This was by design to allow the cows to graze in certain areas while the others grew back after having been eaten. This terraced land rolled down to the edge of the creek where we were standing. The creek itself being maybe 40 feet wide at this point including its rock strewn banks. Now if you were to stand on the western side of the creek your back was to the farm. And if you crossed over to the eastern side your back was now against a somewhat steep embankment with trees of many shapes and sizes growing on it. Standing on this other side facing the farm. If you looked to your right hand side you would see one of the large barns in the distance. Several of these beautiful terraced grass hills spotted with trees and bushes. And the creek would disappear as it went north behind a bend and some trees. The creek had grayish colored sharply angled stones on both of its banks as well as within it. Some were fairly large weighing hundreds of pounds and most of the larger stones within the river had a fish hiding behind them.

For the most part the creek was about a foot deep but there were also some small pools which were perhaps 3 feet deep or so. So there we were fishing in Otter Creek. The day was very overcast and gray which I prefer to fish in rather than bright sunlight so for me it was perfection. And trust me when I tell you that there wasn't another soul in sight. We had permission to be here by the owner and he was away on a Christian mercy mission in South America. Being a doctor by trade he and a medical team occasionally donate their skills and time in an effort to help others who are less fortunate than most of us. So we were alone and tucked down into this creek.

For those of you who don't fish. There are times when we fishermen laugh and joke around but most of the time is spent in silence and solitude. And it was at this time for some 2 or 3 hours that we were quietly working the creek. At some point we both heard a large splash or slap on the water which came from our north side somewhere around this bend that I told you about. I saw my uncle looking in the direction of the splash as did I and we both kept on fishing.

Moments later we heard a couple of more splashes in succession. We were both on the steep eastern side of the creek facing the farm at this time. From the other side we would have had a direct view of the area where we had just heard the splashing. We kind of came together and said to each other quietly. I wonder what that was. Now a splash always gets the utmost attention from a fisherman. And it doesn't matter if you are in the bay, ocean, lake, river or creek. We want to know what's splashing and why. So the two of us very stealthily began to creep along the bank. My uncle being closer to where the splashing had occurred than myself. We both were kind of hunched over trying to catch a first glimpse under some tree branches. When all of a sudden I saw a long dark arm reach down and hit the water. Splash! My uncle had reeled backwards almost falling. He turned and mouthed to me… It's a damn Bigfoot! He waved for me to move back. We must have retreated some 100 yards away to a point far beyond where we had begun. It was then that we crossed to the other side of the creek climbing up the farms first grassy berm to a point where we were now maybe 15 feet or so above the creek bottom. We started to make our way slowly towards where we had seen the creature.

Doing our utmost to use some bushes and small trees as cover we finally came into position where we could see the Bigfoot and hunkered down to observe its movements. We had been previously maybe 90 feet away when I saw the arm. And now we were maybe 250 feet away but we could see everything. As it turns out my uncle had seen allot more than an arm at the same time as me. But his vantage point was slightly better than mine being some 15 feet or so ahead of me on the bank. This Bigfoot must have been so preoccupied with trying to grab a trout that it didn't stand a chance of noticing us before. He was bent over staring at the water without taking so much as a single break to look away. We watched him try to grab a trout maybe 20 times without success and he just kept trying. This thing was determined. Now just in case you don't know trout are extremely slimy. This slime is a protective coating on them and it's generally only after a good fight that you are able to cradle them very gently in your hand and take the hook out of their mouth.

But to me no matter who or what you are the act of just grabbing one swimming would be nearly impossible. Hence the creatures frustration. We must have watched for 45 minutes and it still hadn't had any success in catching a trout. When finally it looked up. Surveyed the area briefly. And turned climbing up the steep bank in 3 steps and having reached the top it walked away out of our sight. The bank it had climbed must have been about 15 feet tall and was on a very steep angle. It was only then that the two of us began to talk quietly. This monster had taken 2 small steps to get out of the river. Just like you or I might being extra careful on the rocky bottom.

At that point is was maybe 2 feet from the inclined embankment. I said to you that the embankments steepest slope was about 15 feet tall. When it was standing next to this embankment for a brief moment. It was well over half the height of this slope. More than likely 9 feet or so tall. And it took 3 strides up this steep embankment having used no hand grabs and was gone over the top walking away out of our sight. It was absolutely out of this world. Now just so you can picture this in your mind's eye. The terrain around here is so undulating that you could more than likely have 20 different people standing in 20 different directions. Each one of them being positioned a 100 yards away from you. And you may not be able to see anyone of them. Initially when I saw the arm come into view. It had to be 5 feet long. It turns out that my uncle had seen the head and upper body at that same time that I had seen the extended arm. So he knew way before I did exactly what it was that we were seeing. Its fur had some rusty colored undertones to it. And I think that if the sun was shining we would have seen more of that in the form of some reddish hues. The fur was actually very long. On some areas of its body and in particular the head. I would say it was 10 inches or so in length and it kind of hung off the back of its arms as well.

The head was somewhat conical but not pointy. The upper part of the skull just stood out much prouder than ours. Its face was much flattened with the jaw somewhat protruding well beyond its nose. Its facial skin was also very much darkened and deeply furrowed with wrinkles. In fact the wrinkles were so deep that they appeared as painted black lines on the face and brow of the creature. When we saw it take the 3 steps upward its legs were obviously flexed to the maximum. The thigh muscles had banged up to the point where they looked to be 2 feet thick in flexion. I am trying to convey to you that they appeared to be the thickness of tree trunks. And the body strength that would be needed to do this so quickly and without grabbing so much as a branch would be off the charts in the human realm. But this thing is in no way a human being nor our offspring in some mutated way. This is some kind of animal. I remember seeing a film clip of a grizzly bear running down a deer on a mountain slope. This grizzly was booking and its musculature was all business. By the way it caught the deer and killed it. When I watch a deer on my own property get spooked and run. It is incomprehensible that anything else could catch it. And yet this huge 1500 lb. grizzly had the wherewithal to do so.

This beast's back was 5 times as thick as the most massive weight lifters that you have ever seen in your life. I would venture to say that it could probably snap a baseball bat in half with just its fingers. Each of the steps which it took on the bank compressed downward about a foot or more of soil under its weight. And it still only took 3 steps to go up 15 feet. Think about that fact for just a moment. If it was just 3 steps with no soil movement. It would be 5 feet per step uphill. But if you now add in the fact that it was actually losing a foot on each step due to soil movement from its downward force and weight. Each step was then at least 6 feet up hill. That is insane if you think about it and it was done as fast as a child skipping on a flat sidewalk. It would be as if I at 6 feet tall.

Could extend my leg to the top of my shoulder taking a step upward. I would say that an estimate of its weight would have to be perhaps 1200 to 1500 lbs. When we had briefly caught a back view of the creature it appeared to me that its triceps area of the arm was maybe 12 inches wide. Perhaps even more than that. Now try standing in front of a mirror while holding a foot long ruler next to your arm and visualize what I am saying. It's was all so real and yet unreal at the same time. Now I know that you and I both get it. But when you are there seeing it with your own two eyes. Then and only then does it ring true and become part of your reality. Well readers I think that Danny just hit one over the wall with that sighting and description. So I will leave well enough alone.

The Wagon Train Diary

The following is a brief but factual excerpt from the diary of Mary Skelton. A diary which was kept while heading west in the early days of our nation. We have been on the trail for many a day now. By my own accounting 59. The men have deemed it necessary to both rest our animals and hunt for a spell. The location being seemingly suitable for both of our needs having settled on good water, grass and ample timber to find their mark… THIS NEXT ENTRY BEGINS 3 DAYS LATER…. WE WILL BEGIN NOW.

Last evening as all were settled down for the nights rest. Many of the gentlemen stood watch by the fire while the women and the children for the most part slept. At the rear was our chuck wagon with our journeys provisions contained within. The men having had good success over the past two days had set to smoke the meat from the previous day's kills. It was the hope of all that it would sustain us until journeys end. As it happened somewhat of a commotion had erupted during the overnight awakening the entirety of the camp. The men knowing that the members of our troop were all accounted for and resting easy. Were surprised by the sudden rocking and the sound of a loud crash emanating from the chuck wagon.

As several of the bravest and stoutest of our men approached the wagons rear. A beast of the most hideous appearance and immense proportions leaped upon them from within the wagon striking one of the men with a fierce blow. As it commenced to scream with the wail of a banshee from hell. The remaining men set loose with their arms prevailing upon the beast and killing the creature dead. As all had been awakened by the ruckus. The entire troop stood gazing at the beast who was laid to waste under the starlit sky. Covered in fur from head to toe and having the appearance of a man beast. It was taller in stature than any man in our group. And wider than an ox when lying down to rest. The hands and feet being in size several times that of our own. The mouth was agape as we viewed the beast's teeth which were broad and somewhat yellowed. Being well worn from apparent age and reason of wear. None would think of making a feast of the creature although the meat was substantial indeed. Not knowing from where it came and being unfamiliar with the breed. We deemed it so to bury the creature where it had come to rest being no small feat in and of itself. The beast being so massive in its dimensions.

✗

The New Brunswick Account

I will now present to you an interesting couple of pages from a 1915 hunter's diary. Which the great grandson had brought to me to read. These were the only pages that I saw which I deemed to be of interest. And I am sure that you will find them more than interesting as well. New Brunswick last fall Nov.1-15 Maple Grove S.W. Mirimichi River camp. The owner and his brother as cook. With two other guides comprised the working side of our party. David Riis, myself and David Hindsley were on the paying end. We began in Chicago with layovers in Toronto, Montreal and Quebec.

Arriving at Maple Grove Nov.1. Upon leaving Maple Grove there was nearly a 20 mile hike to reach the rivers camp which we accomplished in one days' time on horseback. As the cook prepared our meal and while the guides were hitching our teams. We began to scout finding numerous moose, deer and bear tracks. As well as several unidentified tracks of a large nature in the fresh snow. Between the camp and the Taxis River our troop had gotten the jump on three deer. Two does and one buck. We bagged the buck and the does were left to run. During the first few days at camp. We had seen numerous cow moose and many deer. And David with one guide in tow became the laughing stock of the camp. When he and the guide returned with a tale of a large hair covered naked man seen darting through the trees. Many of the beasts while there. Were too far away so we held our fire.

I bagged a nice bull using my 30-06 hollow point. A bullet which performed excellently on the deer and moose. And I used the 280 Ross 160 gr. hollow point on another bull penetrating the abdomen. The bull travelled some 1 mile before we caught him. Finishing him off with two more slugs. David had used the 30-06 Remington 180 grain cartridge placing several shots through another bulls broadside. After which he ran some 100 yards and dropped. Hindsley had an opportunity at another bull but passed because its head was not to his liking. Total game seen 20 moose 14 of which were cows 3 bulls 3 calves 35 deer 1 hairy man.

✗

The Travelers Diary

This excerpt was taken from a travelers diary purchased at an estate sale. Its origins being from the 1800s and the writers name is believed to be Reinhardt Geffe. In the course of our travels through Oregon. We learned the history of many of the men we met. The opportunities which the country gives may be learned in the results from individual cases. Bearing in mind that the earliest settlers entered the state in or after 1849. And the majority of these men have achieved their present position in from fifteen to eight years back from the present time.

I will begin with a gentleman who, to use his own words, bought a farm seven years ago. This was because he found it impossible to both bring up and educate a rising family on a salary of 1000.00 per year as a Presbyterian minister. His estate consists of 500 acres of land which is lying on the slope of the coast range towards the Willamette Valley. And varies in character being partly hill land and partly bottom. Six years ago when he entered on farming. He was 120.00 dollars in debt after he had bought his land. It has long since been entirely free. He was utterly ignorant of the business when he began.

And was content for three years to imitate his neighbors, ploughing, sowing and harvesting when they did. He learned by degrees to walk alone having lost his two sons in the most hideous of events thought possible to man. He said that he had now ventured to bring into cultivation much land that his predecessor had thought worthless for wheat. Land which this year was producing from fifteen to twenty five bushels per acre. While much of his wheat land yielded from forty to fifty bushels of the same. But his general average having been brought down to twenty five bushels by the new land and by some marshy soil which he had not yet found time to drain. He has a very comfortable eight room house. And a splendid orchard of twelve acres which is full of fruit trees.

This gentleman of English parentage and education told us that he had enjoyed life to the fullest. When some years back he had fallen prey to a great depression brought about by some demons from hell. His children being two boys and three girls. And his wife having died in child birth of the last. He said that while working the harvest. He, his two young sons and three hired hands were in the fields. The sons being mainly involved in more play than any work of sorts. Being not of age for strenuous activities. When one of the hands had sighted from some distance. Not one but two of what he described as behemoth proportioned hairy men running from the wood line across the wheat field towards his sons. Having reached the youths and seized upon them. The beasts from hell were seen retreating back to the wood line with the speed of a horse in full gallop. Carrying the boys kicking and screaming under their arms. By the time the help had reached the gentleman and he had gathered his wits. Some time had passed. The four men had retrieved a shotgun and rifles and commenced to follow the trail through the now parted wheat into the trees. In swift pursuit of the hairy man beasts. When after having searched for hours and nothing could be seen or heard.

A posse of some twenty five locals was assembled which headed back into the forest on horseback. As the next three days were coming to a close. Many more men and women having joined the search. The trackers had come upon a trail of great prints which led them to a scene of horrific carnage beneath the pines. The youths were discovered sprawled over the high boughs of a pine. Many, many miles from the gentlemen's farmstead. After much to do to both climb the pine and retrieve the bodies. They were seen to be torn apart with many large pieces missing from the apparent bites of these flesh eating hairy demons. The help having said that these demons were covered in fur like that of a bear. And were of the greatest stature and girth. Who seemed to spirit themselves across the field with the greatest of speed and dexterity. The wheat after which appearing as though it had been parted by a horse cart where they had travelled. The gentleman being a local Presbyter. Laid to rest his only sons with the community by his side.

X

The Fur Trappers Evidence

As you continue to read these tales. My initial query was that of inviting fisherman, hunters and hikers to contact me. I was looking for those who had either seen a Bigfoot or had believed to have found evidence of the beast's existence. The variety of those who have contacted me is unending. Many of which did not fit the description of my initial request but felt it necessary to contact me never the less. Here is the account of Peter Edwards. A fourth generation fur trapper from southeast Alaska. I do ask all of those whom I interview to bring as much detail as possible to you the reader. In an effort to fully develop the happenings surrounding their personal encounter or evidential findings.

Here is what Peter had to share. My family has been in Alaska for over 100 years. My great grandfather had first come here in hopes of finding gold. And although he did find some gold he found himself secondarily learning the craft of setting traps and snares to acquire pelts and furs. Which in and of itself can be quite profitable for a well-schooled trapper.

Back in my great grandads day there were not many regulations up here or those who enforced them with rigor. As for myself there are a number of critters that I trap throughout the seasons. But it is around the trapping of the martens that this story which I share had come to pass. If you are unaware the Marten is more commonly known by fur coat buyers as sable. They have a beautiful and extremely soft coat of generally reddish brown fur. And depending on the markets prices these pelts can be quite profitable. Each year I bring in between 100 and sometimes north of 200 marten pelts. Now the real trick in trapping a marten is to find their habitat and locate the animal's specific territories. If you have done your homework and provide the right baits to lure them in. The animal's generally curious characteristics will virtually assure you of capturing them.

Martens like their solitude. And they prefer to stay in piney forests. This is because their favorite food is the pine squirrel. But they have a taste for many other things as well such as hares and ptarmigan. So if you are going to bait well you must also hunt for their favorites with great efficiency also. And it is really more in tracking the marten's prey that you will uncover the marten's habitat. Find the food source and you will find the consumer of that food. There are two ways to capture a marten. They can either be caught above the ground or on the ground itself. And this obviously requires two independent styles of traps. On the ground in these days and times we use what's known as a Combo Box- Connibear set. And off the ground we use a leaning pole set which will also requires a nice stiff branch. One can also use a foothold trap but the modern Connibear works quite well. Martens don't seem to be quite that aggressive as hunters and their diet seems to be rather broad. There are many preferred baits such as the ones I mentioned already. But it was the beaver which great grandad loved to use. However my bait of choice based on the ease of my attaining it is fish and of course all of the rest when I can get them. I generally add a bit of skunk essence to any of my baits in order to spice them up. If it stinks they will come.

One of my choice areas is that of Granite Creek. And it is in this very location that my findings came to be. More often than not I will set my trap string over quite a long distance. This business of trapping is not for the weak. Because depending on the density of their population in different regions. You may be fortunate to catch a marten or two for every mile of trap line or so that you set. So you can begin to do the math of the type of effort and hiking involved in setting ones trap line. And by the way you are not walking down a paved sidewalk. It can be difficult terrain to navigate on foot. I also keep a detailed log as to the whereabouts of my traps and what was taken from each one year to year. What I had sent to you was a copy of such a log before we met. I must interject here for a moment my readers. Yes it is me the author. The detail in Peters log was incredible. And it was from this very log that the details and findings which you will soon read were taken. And now back to Peters account. My routine is to put out a set of approximately 10 traps. The location of these placements is based on several factors. The first being locating marten tracks whenever possible. This method being much easier in snowy seasons.

The second being finding available food sources. In particular the pine squirrels. And vegetation is a must whenever and wherever it can be found in conjunction with the other criteria. My most productive traps are more often located near the zones where swamp meets timber or wherever a river meets the timberline. So I had gone about setting my line in the usual fashion. And later on in the week I had returned to check the traps. I should mention one more thing before going on that I had forgotten. On some of my traps. The pole sets in particular. Which are the ones I generally set by timberlines. I will hang the shiny lid of a tin can. This is a trick my grandad passed on to me. The martens are quite inquisitive. And the sunlight and or moonlight reflecting off of these lids seems to draw them in.

As I was saying I had gone back to check my set and everything was fine until I got to the ones located by the timberline. This area has some low lying hills running up to the timber. With a fair amount of varied and well dispersed vegetation being present. I had seen a large population of hares and pine squirrels working in this area and I had actually set three traps in a one mile span because it looked so promising. In general one trap per mile is typical for me. When I came upon the first pole set it was ripped apart and the trap had been sprung. Something which is very hard to do without the use of hands.

I could tell that a marten had been caught in it because of the blood on it. So something or someone had stolen my marten. This really got me aggravated because men can and do rip off trapper's catches. When I approached the second trap I was shocked to see that the same thing had occurred and now I was really mad. This was by the way the first time I had ever come across such a phenomena. The rest of the traps were not tampered with and I had actually done quite well. So all the traps having been reset and baited I finished my loop and went back. The next time coming back in to check them I was met with the grim realization that all of my timberline traps had been opened. Each one of them had caught a marten and all of the martens had been stolen. Now three out of three traps having caught something is damn near impossible. But three out of three traps being found opened and the catch removed is beyond impossible. It wasn't until I had made it all the way down by the marshes edge that my eyes began to be opened as to what was going on. The marsh trap was set just inside of a soft area coming off the hard pack next to it. It was next to it that I saw some very large water soaked impressions in the muddy soil. Now there was no way of telling what type of tracks they were because they were basically large muddy depressions filled with water. My first impression was that it was a bear. And this trap also had captured a marten which was now gone like the others.

I had never experienced such a thing before. The only thing I had ever come across or seen was evidence of a lynx or fox having torn at the flesh of a marten while it was snared in the trap. But never had I ever come across opened traps with the prey completely removed from them. This was most unusual so I decided I was going to place two bear traps near the marten traps. I would conceal them totally and post them into the earth to secure them. These bear traps would require a considerable weight to trigger them. If there was in fact a bear coming to my traps I would get it. The first time back through my set with the added bear traps nothing was awry and I had gotten four martens. So all was reset and baited in the same way I had always done.

It was on the following check that things got a little weird. And this is why you and I came in contact with each other. I had actually believed that after seeing the previous set untouched that all was well. And whatever or whoever had robbed my catch before had moved on but that was about to change. When I reached the second bear trap my set was destroyed and the bear trap was not only sprung but it was empty and had been forced on edge into the ground. It was actually jammed into the ground some 5 or 6 inches. Not an easy thing to do with a wide steel object weighing some 20 or 30 lbs. I examined it and saw blood. So something got caught by it and had escaped. And that in and of itself is beyond belief. It was when I started to look around for further evidence that my eye caught something lying about 3 feet from where the trap had been set. The trap having been moved some 20 feet to the place where it was shoved into the earth.

I thought at first that it was a bloody portion of a large furry paw which had been sheared off in the bear trap. But upon closer inspection it was not a paw at all but rather a fur covered segment of a large human like foot. It appeared to be from the mid foot forward having been cut or torn on an angle including what were four large and very wide toes. I flipped it over with a stick and saw that the sole was flat and leathery. But here's the really odd thing. It had no claws just thick and nasty looking nails. Each of the four toes was between 2 ½ to 3 inches wide. They were very thick and about 3 inches long. I knew it wasn't a bear's foot and it certainly hadn't come from a human. The only thought that had crossed my mind virtually immediately was that it belonged to a Sasquatch.

So I set about to do a little tracking. There was still some snow around but most of the area was open and completely devoid of snow. I was following the trail of blood which brought me into the timber where I found more. There were still some patches of snow where I could see large footprints. One from the bloodied chopped off foot and the other print being normal. This thing must have been in incredible pain and limping badly when leaving this site. And who knows where it was going and if it would survive infection and or anything else that would occur from such a wound. This was a large piece of its foot that had been sheared off. I could see that the other undamaged foot was about 22 or so inches long and maybe 10 inches wide. And I dared not follow any further especially unarmed in pursuit of a wounded monster. Since that day's events I have not placed any trap sets there again.

✗

The Medora Monster

This tale was told to me by Abe Silverman who hailed from the vicinity of Chicago Illinois. He and his friends had gone to do a little fishing and caught something they weren't expecting. Here is Abe Silverman's account. I and two of my friends had been to this camp in Medora before. The last time was for a moose hunt. And this time around we were sampling the fantastic fishing which we were made aware of on the last outing several years back. It was 1958 that we headed back up north to an area by Sulfide Lake in Northern Saskatchewan. The only way in and out of this location was by float plane which is quite a thrill in and of itself for a couple of city guys. When we first spoke you had asked me to be inclusive of any details so I thought you would enjoy these old brochure prices. It is remarkable how things have changed. But mind you this was an extremely expensive undertaking back in 58.

We would be staying in what was advertised as a light housekeeping cabin equipped with a propane stove and a refrigerator. There was quick freezing and ice available. We were responsible to bring a bedroll and our own groceries. The cabins ran for 5 dollars a day per person. With a 10 dollar minimum. Special family rates were available. Boat rentals were 7 dollars a day and 9 dollars a day for a motor with fuel if you didn't want to row. A guide could be at your disposal for 15 dollars per day. But there was a package deal as well. If you were a party of 3 or more persons which we were. Fifteen bucks a day for everyone bought you the cabin, boat, motor and guide. The flying being the only additional cost. And I think the float plane cost 35 bucks at the time. They had a two-way radio at this outpost as a form of communication.

And just as a point of amusement. When we had gone for moose several years back it was 300 dollars a week per person including an all-day wilderness guide. And that was if you bagged a moose. If you hadn't bagged one the price was reduced to 250 dollars per week. Now that is really funny to look back on considering that this type of trip today would be somewhere north of 7 grand at the very least. The cabin also was very neat being made in the traditional way out of real logs. It was constructed on about 4 or 5 foot tall piers and had about 6 steps leading up to the front door. The fish that this area boasts about are the walleye, northerns, rainbows and lake trout. And man oh man are they big and beautiful up there. Every day we were up early and fishing the lake. Our tackle consisted mainly of light spinning gear and spoons. Red and white being the most productive pattern. We were occasionally using some top water plugs for a little surface action. But with the spoons it was literally one fish after another being taken. And it didn't matter at all where we went on the lake. The fishing was just incredible. We were landing some trout that were over 30 inches in length and the fight on light tackle was outstanding to say the least.

I think it was on or about the third or fourth day of fishing. That we decided by recommendation of our guide to take a little boat ride to the northeast section of the lake in order to check on the action over there. He also said that this was a very beautiful part of the lake and its surrounding terrain. We had already actually seen several moose over the previous days eating at the lakes shore. It was as we were rounding a bend in the lake when the guide pointed out what he believed to be a moose swimming across the lake. Now to us city boys who knew that moose swam. But there it was or so we thought. He moved a little closer and then stopped the motor so as not to frighten it. The creature was about 150 yards from where it had presumably began its swim entering the water. And it was still at least 400 yards from where it seemed to be heading. Now that's a fairly good swim in anyone's book. I would say that we were about 200 yards away when he stopped the engine and there we sat. There was no wind and no current in this still body of water. There was visibly a large wake emanating from behind the animal and all that we could see was a large dark head protruding over the top of the lake as it swam. We were mesmerized by the sight. I guess it was when it came about 75 yards from shore that things started to get real interesting.

For it was then that this animal must have come into some shallower water where its body became partly visible because now it was able to touch the lakes bottom and begin walking. But as the body came into view it was not that of a cow moose at all. In fact it wasn't even on four legs. It was of humanlike stature with maybe 30% of its body above the lakes surface. It was then that we realized it was also turning its head towards us from time to time. We could clearly see arm swing that was very slight because most of its arms were still in the water. It was just like you or I would appear when walking in waist or chest deep water in a pool. A little bit into the walk the water must have become deeper again. So we continued watching as it was once again in the water swimming. It wasn't until it was maybe 20 or 30 feet from the lakes edge that it completely emerged in full sight of us from the water and I could see it turn its head one last time to look at us.

And then it walked straight away into the woods. When I tell you that we were absolutely blown away by what we saw that would be an understatement. Our guide was scratching his head in disbelief. He said to us that he couldn't believe that we had just seen a Sasquatch. This was what the local Indians had always called these things. But he had never believed in them never encountering one for himself. About 20 minutes after it had walked into the woods we motored into the vicinity where it had been. But to a man nobody was willing to get very close. And certainly we weren't getting out of the boat to have a look around. There was one large bough protruding from a pine that I had seen its head pass in front of. And when we got closer it was then that I realized that this beast was about 10 feet tall. A point which I made to the fellas in the boat over and over again. We could see a couple of depressions on the shore from its feet but we were not going to go any closer to get a better look at them.

It was fully in appearance like a giant hairy human. But the bodily dimensions were staggering. There was only a very short shoreline where it came out of the lake if you could even call it a shore. Maybe 4 feet wide at best. From the yardage we were away and now being there. This things body was about as thick front to back as the beach was wide. I am talking maybe 3 feet thick. And knowing that its head had gone by this branch which I was now relatively speaking very close to us. It was more than likely 10 feet tall or more. The one wet footprint was right at the edge of the water. And the second was just shy of the brush. So its stride was about 5 feet. It didn't even stop for a blink after having swum some 600 yards. It simply had emerged and began walking away in a very casual matter of fact motion into the woods.

Why it would swim the lake rather than walk around through the woods is anyone's guess. It was difficult to see great detail with so little time. But it was most definitely from our viewpoint completely covered in dark fur. I saw nothing to indicate white skin on the face or anywhere else on its entire body for that matter. I would have to say that in my opinion the legs were shorter than the upper body. And having said as much the arms which hands swung below the knee must have been 7 feet long. The other thing of note is this. Even though we only saw it walk briefly it appeared kind of wobbly at the knees. Either that or it had somewhat of a knock knee disposition. It was very hard to judge. We headed back to the cabin in the boat and as you can well imagine the conversation that afternoon and evening was incredible to say the least. It was something that none of us will certainly ever forget.

✗

The Howler

This account was presented to me by Ron Witherspoon a resident of the Pacific Northwest. And believe me when I tell you. That's as close as you will get with Ron to telling you where he likes to fish. I had hiked into one of my usual fly fishing haunts with my lab Ruby. And if you're wondering why I am not more forthcoming with specifics about my location. There was nobody there the last time I fished. And I don't want to see anyone there the next time I fish there either.

People have a grand way of lousing up a good thing. I had set up camp on my usual bend in the river. A location where a nice rocky tributary tails off the side of the main river. This spot is nestled in a valley which is flanked by two mountains on either side. And more of the same being located to the northwest. A setting which is typical of many of the ranges out here in these parts. The first third of the mountains bases being generally covered with grass, brush and stands of pines. I had made camp on a nice dry spot near the river's edge. And set down with Ruby for a spell to prepare my rod and flies. Ruby is a great companion and although she occasionally gets a little rambunctious trying to get the jump on a trout in the stream. All in all I would rather have her with me than be without her. She also gets extremely antsy when she hones in on a predator or any other animal for that matter in our vicinity. Which is fine by me especially when you're out in this country alone.

It was our second day on the river together and the weather was picture perfect. Puffy white cumulous clouds were drifting over the peaks and I could see their shadows sliding over the valleys floor. It must have been about 1 p.m. when Ruby started to growl. She sat down and stared at the mountainside in front of us. She was growling and puffing her mouth up. I was looking in the direction she was and saw nothing but I wear glasses and she doesn't. So who knows what she was seeing. For all I knew it was a rabbit hopping around on the mountainside. But she was unrelenting with the ongoing growling and puffing of her jowls. And still I could not see a thing moving on the entire mountainside. There were several large stands of fir that I could see and a fair amount of patchy thicket. But none of them revealed any clues to my eyes as to why she was on edge. Then suddenly she started to bark. And I was saying to her what do you see girl? What do you see?

It was immediately after I said those words that she started to really bark and would not stop. It got to the point where she was actually howling. All of you dog lovers know of what I speak. And when she had begun this barking and howling a roaring type of howl that is beyond description starting ringing out through the canyon. When this happened she hunkered down on the ground and started to kind of whimper while still staring at the mountain. But now she was crouched completely on the ground. This howl was reverberating throughout the entire valley. It was so deep and long that all I can say to you having been there was that you could actually feel it.

I had heard grizzlies roar on many occasions and this was no grizzly bear that was roaring. And still I couldn't see anything. The truth be told I wasn't even sure from what direction it was coming. But Ruby kept looking straight ahead of our position. I didn't know what to think or do. I just squatted next to Ruby and kept petting and talking to her. Trying to calm her down because she was really upset panting and everything else. A few moments later maybe 5 minutes after this howling roar had stopped. A figure emerged from the firs on the mountainside. It was maybe a thousand yards away and perhaps a good deal more in my estimation. It was making its way along the side of the mountain standing on and walking on two legs completely upright.

I knew immediately that this was not and could not be a man. First of all I had never seen another human being here. Let alone a human walking the side of the mountain covered from head to toe in black. And this after hearing a roar that could have knocked you down if it had happened next to you. I was convinced that whatever I was looking at was the same creature that had made the howling roar only minutes beforehand. And Ruby started to bark again like crazy. She was barking and growling while hopping up and down on her front legs. This creature was casually strutting across the base heading directly for another stand of furs to the north. I stood there in utter amazement at what I was looking at. It was very tall and thick that much I knew. Because I had seen many bears at the same distance and against the same type of backdrop. And this thing dwarfed a bear for sure. There is no question that it was walking and its arms were swinging back and forth just like ours do when we walk. After it had made the other stand and was once again out of my sight. I made an immediate decision to break camp and head on out of there. No way and no how was I going to spend another night with whatever that was prowling around the area while I slept. And that is what I saw and heard that day on the river.

✗

The Pheasant Hunters

Eddie Pettigrew came to me with a rather amazing story which I am about to share with you. And now here is Eddie with his account. I and some of the good old boys had planned a weekend pheasant hunt. If everyone showed up who was supposed to come we would have 12 men. A grouping of men that would be perfect to flush the soybean field that we had in mind for the days hunt. It was Saturday at about 10 a.m. by the time all of these old timers arrived. I was the captain of the hunt and my job was to call out when I wanted the two end men to begin the flush through the field. When everything works well the line of hunters will form a crescent moving forward through the field. Which gives the end men a shot at anything flying away. Most of the guys including myself were shooting 8 shot through a modified choke. This shot size and choke would put a good spread of pellets on any bird at 20 to 25 yards. Since the pheasant typically is a low flyer you won't have much more time or distance to shoot than that without endangering those of course who are flanking you on the drive. The rule is that we never turn more than the 10 and 2 o'clock position with our bodies or our guns. That day we had taken about 13 birds which was a fairly good day's work for the crew. The next day we were supposed to hit a nearby corn field for more of the same but the weather wasn't cooperating.

The forecast was for rain showers all day long. I got on the phone with my buddy Mike and asked him if he was willing to give it a go anyway. All of the other guys having bailed out on the phone chain. I told Mike that I really liked the look of the thicket next to the soybean field we were at yesterday. And I suggested bringing the dog with us to work it. Mike was usually game for anything, anywhere and anytime and today was no exception. I put my setter in the truck and met up with him at the field. It was really dreary and drizzling when we got there. Now just so you understand there was thicket flanking this field on two sides. It was a very deep and intertwined bramble. And I am here to tell you that there was no way a man would penetrate it or attempt to do so in his right mind. You would be torn up before you knew what hit you. But for a dog they could sneak around low going in and out of the little tunnels that were formed by the growth.

As much as this had appeared to me to be choice ground. The morning didn't work out so well. I don't know if it was the rain or the fact that the temperature had dropped ten degrees but the dog hadn't spooked a single bird. I thought that maybe he couldn't get to where they were hunkered down and they were just staying put. Knowing from experience that a bird will not jump until they are forced to. Many times you almost have to step on them before they will take to the air. Having had no success in the morning we took a little break. Our plan being after break to hit the other side of the field. The rain having let up we thought we might have a better go of it in the afternoon. So we took the dog and walked about a half mile over to the other thicket. This one was even denser than the other had been and I began to wonder if the dog could even work it at all. We began to work southward as the dog moved through the mess. After about 20 minutes the dog was deep inside to the point that we couldn't even see or hear him so I called him out. We petted him and gave him a snack before sending him back in. It must have been only a few minutes when we heard him yelp and start to bark frantically. We thought that perhaps he had found a bobcat because that was the only other time I had heard him sound like this.

Now for today's hunt I had switched my ammo to a 7 ½ shot. The theory being that shooting over this thicket which was very deep. The 7 ½ shot would give me a range of about 30 to 35 yards which is better than the 8 shot. The pellets being slightly larger and heavier giving them more flight time to the target. So the dog is barking frantically in the thicket and he is not responding to my call at all. When all of a sudden erupting out of the top and running through the thicket is this monstrous Bigfoot. We both knew immediately what it was. I turned my over and under double at it and hit it squarely with both loads at maybe 20 yards if that. It was very close. The dog was going berserk at the same time it had jumped out of the thicket. He had obviously already seen what we could not. I'm not bragging but I am a very proficient shot and I nailed this critter broadside with both barrels and he didn't even flinch. Now running through this patch would be like you or I trying to pull free from a pair of razor blade handcuffs. And he was bowling through this shit like he was running through a wheat field. My partner had quickly squeezed off two more rounds but unfortunately by that time it wasn't worth the effort. If my two loads didn't take him down at 20 yards nothing would.

In about thirty seconds flat he was gone goodbye. We tried to hustle running down the thicket. Mike had 3 more chambered and I was trying to reload but it was all to no avail. This booger was gone and we were shocked that we couldn't even see him running away anywhere. Talk about excitement. We had gone from zero to hero and back in all of about 45 second's total. My heart was racing a mile a minute and I know Mike felt the same way. We both kept saying to each other that we couldn't believe it. But believe it we did. We had just witnessed and shot at a giant booger in the soybean field's thicket. This sucker was easily 9 or more feet tall. Because no matter where you stood by the side of this thicket it was a foot taller than me and I am nearly 6 foot.

And this critter was a full 2 feet or more head and shoulders out of the top. He was kind of grayish white and his fur was longer than I thought it would be having heard all of the stories beforehand. The upper body looked like two fifty gallon drums welded together. He took one fast glance at us and tore out. I don't know how or what they are made out of but if you or I attempted to do what it did you couldn't. It would take you 10 minutes to go 10 feet. And you would be so cut up we would have to call an ambulance. It was tearing through this mess at full bore giddy up like a weed whacker on steroids. Sometime after all this I couldn't stop thinking about the shotgun blasts showing no effect on the creature. And I got to think that maybe its skin is like an elephants. And perhaps its hair follicles go in a couple of inches or something. I mean a shotgun won't take an elephant down and it wouldn't take this booger down either. When we got back to town we told all the boys what we had seen and they were beside themselves. This things outer skin must be as thick as a board. I hit him squarely with close to 1200 pellets at 50 to 60 feet. To be honest with you I didn't even notice a clump of fur come flying off. I mean nothing. It was like I fired 2 blanks at it. When I briefly saw its face I thought of an Indian chief. I don't know exactly why I say that but it was my impression at that moment in time. I tell you what. You do not want to run into one of these bad boys with anything less than a 30/06 and that's the truth of the whole matter. Well readers it sounds like the old booger gave the boys a run for their money doesn't it?

✗

The Greenhouse Evidence

Max and Marissa Vandergroff came to me with some rather unusual and telling evidence which I believe you will find very interesting. They were living at the time north of Newport Vermont near the Canadian border. Here is their story. I wouldn't say at that time in our lives that my wife and I were full fledge homesteaders but we were certainly very self-sufficient. And we lived this lifestyle not so much out of necessity but rather because we enjoyed the activities and the rewards associated with them.

My wife was making some money with a mail order rubber stamp business and I was engaged in more than my fair share of mechanic work for many of the locals and beyond. I had an old bread truck equipped with mostly everything that I would need shy of having to get the parts. The best part of my work being that I made my own hours and determined when I would work or not. We had purchased the home we were living in for believe it or not 1800 dollars cash. And it came with 5 acres of property which at the time of sale had already been cleared for the most part.

I also bought an old tractor from a local farmer and a couple of attachments to go along with it. I guess it was over the course of about the next 3 years or so that we had constructed a pig pen. A fairly good size chicken coop. And we had put up 3 large green houses building one per year and not starting the next until the first was up and running. The 3 of them being equally 20 x 40 feet. We also had wood burning furnaces to pump some heat into the greenhouses. But the reality was that you could only use them to get things going in the early spring. The temperatures being too cold to keep them warm prior to that time of the year. Our bills at that time were so insignificant in comparison to what we made and what we actually needed to buy. That we wanted for nothing. We were doing very well for ourselves. We had learned both on our own and through the help of many locals through the years how to better our homestead. And how to get the most out of what we were doing whether it be the pigs, chickens or the greenhouses.

With everything we were doing we still had the need to buy a fair amount of things. And just so you understand we were not wiping our butts with leaves in the woods by any means. We had electricity and running water with plumbing just like most of America. One day my wife had gone out to get some eggs when she realized that a large section of chicken wire had been torn from the coops fence. She also noticed a good deal of feathers and blood around the coop on the ground. Which meant that something had broken into the coop and gotten to some of our birds. I think it was in late April when this had occurred. When I came home later that day from a repair job the two of us went out to survey the damage. Whatever had done this had good strength. I say this because the wire had been applied to the 6 x 6 posts with 1" deep staples. The kind that are hammered in. Many of them having been pulled loose in the process and a fair amount of the wire having been ripped away leaving the staples behind. The fact being that if you or I were to try doing the same we would achieve nothing except getting cuts and lacerations. It was that tough. After I had made the repair and taken a head count of birds lost.

Three chickens had been taken. I had never seen a bear here before but what else could I think other than that a bear had done this. So the two of us started looking around for tracks or further evidence. It was then that we started to notice some large flat impressions. I wouldn't call them footprints because the ground was much too hard. But I will say that they appeared like tamped flat spots on the ground. Kind of like when one is tamping gravel for a new walkway. I think it was perhaps a week later when the hen house had been ravaged yet again during the night. My wife having discovered it in the same way she had the previous week. The wire had once again been ripped off the posts. And this time a section of the plywood house had been torn away and most of the eggs were gone or broken inside of the coop. Broken shells and yolks were scattered all over the place. This time we had a little bit of a trail to follow. Because whatever had tried to carry these eggs away had broken or lost most of them in the process. We could follow this trail into the edge of the woods but no further.

I consulted with a few of my neighbors who were big time hunters. Who in the end were all in agreement that I had a bear problem. And that I could either trap it or kill it. Either way all of them thought it would just keep coming back for the chickens and maybe for the pigs sooner than later. So my neighbor Ernie gave me an old bear trap which I baited with some raw thawed pork. My wife and I decided to sit up all night for however many days it would take to get this thing. We were sitting near a back picture window from which we could see the coop. The room next to us had hand crank casement windows and a door leading outside into the yard. My thoughts were that when we saw the bear I would first try to get a shot off through the casement window cranked wide open. If not I would then gently swing the door open and try the same. That was my plan. On the first night we actually saw a fox surveying the meat in the trap. It was trying to cautiously reach its snout over the trap and take a bite. But for some reason it was afraid to commit fully and wandered off having eaten nothing. On the second nights watch absolutely nothing at all had happened. But that same day when my wife went out to check on the greenhouses the back end of one of the houses was torn open. It looked like something had opened the door and forced its way through the frame because it was too big to walk through. At least that was my impression at the time. And all of this having happened while we were awake and watching the coop. Albeit this spot was probably 50 yards or so from where we were sitting. And we couldn't see that end of the greenhouse from where we were either. The two of us having heard nothing in the process.

When we went inside there were gigantic footprints within the vegetable beds throughout the entire greenhouse. The beds being constructed of 2 x 12 boards on edge. We had staked them with metal every 4 feet for strength and they were filled with the softest loamiest soil you could imagine. Why a grasshopper could have left a footprint in here. Whatever had walked through here had pulled out most of the small plants and eaten them. Its weight had compressed the loam down to its base which was about 12 to 14 inches total. The prints were perfectly formed from gigantic human like feet. The difference being the shaping of the toes which were very broad and angled kind of funny. Just so you understand each greenhouses had 6 boxes in them that were 6 x 12 feet. In between these boxes were pea gravel pathways to walk on when you were tending to the vegetables.

Whatever this animal was had walked right into the beds grabbing whatever it wanted and left. I called in the local game warden who when he had arrived and saw what was done was speechless. He was young and all he could say was that it looked like a giant walked through here. Later that morning I had called some of the men over to have a look see and one fellow named George who was an old-timer in the area. Said that he wouldn't have believed it if he hadn't seen it with his own eyes. But it looks to be the work of the Hairy Man of the Woods. He then went on to speak of people in these parts talking about a giant gorilla or hair covered man who had attacked people and killed live stock in days gone by. But none of them had heard of or seen anything of the sort in their lifetimes. And George started saying that whatever this is it needs to be put down and put down now. We were all in agreement. And with feet that size we could only imagine what the rest of it would look like. So together we had devised a plan. One of the boys had a Winnebago mobile home. The plan was to leave everything else in the yard as it had always been including the now damaged greenhouse.

We were going to station the mobile home in the yard where all aspects of the greenhouses, the pen and the coop could be seen for the most part. We would then stake out the property from within the Winnebago with our rifles at the ready. And so it was that we began by bringing over the mobile home and parking it well back into my property. The men were all fired up at this point and everyone wanted to be in on the action. Two days later we were dressed for hunting in the truck. We had the louvered windows open and the door ajar. In the middle of the night one of the guys pointed towards the pig pen saying nothing. The pig pen was most visible from the Winnebago's door. Which as fate would have it was the hardest part of the vehicle to see from. But he could see and that was enough for now.

We were all trying to get some kind of look toward the pen which was almost completely devoid of any light from the back of the house. As I focused my eyes I could make out the pigs with their lightly colored skin all huddled together on one end of the pen. Something they would only do when trying to escape from a predator. And then I saw a large dark mass come into view at the same time they all ran to the other side of the pen out of our view. Ernie was mouthing the words…It's there let's go!

While pointing his finger emphatically at the pen. So we jumped out and Ernie fired the first shot. Then I and Joe Hollander followed. When we all were out is was like the 4th of July. We must have shot 30 rounds into the darkness. Ernie was certain that he had made his mark with the first shot. He said he had his sight right on it at 30 yards distance. We all looked around for blood or anything to indicate it was hit and found none. The next day I did find some blood on the ground right where Ernie had said he hit his mark. He was firing an M1 circa the Korean conflict and one would think that had to hurt at 30 yards. The pen had a fence around it that was 6 feet tall. And the black mass that I had seen was at least 4 or 5 feet taller than the top of the fence and appeared to be very large in every sense of the word.

We had all been hoping for a scenario where several guys would put the hurt on it without a doubt. But as it turned out the first guy out of this small door was going to have the only shot worth taking. Especially when you're shooting in the dark at something that is dark itself. At any rate all of the activity around our house ceased after that night so we were successful with or without seeing a dead body. I filed a report with the warden as to what we had devised and done. He was a little peeved about us firing in the dark at an unknown target. But all is well that ends well I guess and it did end well. Well my readers that is a Bigfoot encounter for the record book. It will make you think twice the next time you're in the greenhouse alone.

✗

Ziggy Stardust

Trevor Riley and his wife Sarah brought this amazing sighting to my attention last spring. Here is what Trevor had to say. Although I swore never to speak of exactly where we were when this took place. I am free to tell you that we were in Idaho at the time. My wife and I had a favorite little picnic area that we frequented. It was a little getaway where we could drive in cook up some dogs and burgers and walk around a little in the woods enjoying nature and each other's company. On one of these outings I had my old boom box out as we usually did sitting on the tailgate of the truck. We were playing some old David Bowie. Ziggy Stardust to be more exact. As the music was playing and we were munching out. A fellow came walking by and said to my wife and I. I love your music guys. My wife said are you a Bowie fan? He said I am the biggest Bowie fan alive. So we invited him over for a beer and a dog. His name was Charlie and we soon found out that he was retired from the railroad and now living out here on a pension.

As the conversation progressed we found out that he had come from the Tri- State area as did we. He then asked us if we had ever seen Bowie live. We told him that we had seen him once during the seventies in the winter at Radio City. And he said no kidding! I was there myself at that very same show. Ziggy Stardust and the Spiders from Mars. We started laughing and reminiscing about that night and the lifestyles we were living at the time. Now what are the odds of people from the same area having seen the same show bumping into each other in Idaho over 40 years later? It was kind of freaky but very cool. So we were bullshitting and eating for about an hour when the conversation took an unexpected turn. We had been talking about our mutual love for the wilderness and this countryside in particular. When Charlie said I do allot of hiking up north hunting for Bigfoot. Well my wife and I glanced at each other like this dude had dropped too many hits of acid.

But he was persistent and quite sincere in his speech so we listened. He asked us what we thought of the whole Bigfoot thing and if we believed they were in fact real. Trevor and I glanced at each other and we told him that I guess we hadn't really thought about it that much. It was then that Trevor said to him what about you? Have you seen any? Well let me tell you we had no idea the can of worms that we had just opened in asking that question.

He pulled out his IPod and started showing us pictures and even some live video he had taken. It was incredible. And again I cannot emphasize enough the dude's sincerity and forthrightness about this whole deal. The stills and video were outstanding. He said that he spends about 2 months out of the year… that is to say a day at a time. Exploring and hiking around the same area. He learned to look for the signs of their habitations. Basically coming to the understanding of how they live and what they do. And he was at the point now where he felt that they knew him and were alright with him being around. Now I know that you and most people immediately take the jump that the photos and everything else today are staged or manipulated on the computer as did we. But when we asked him if he sees them on a regular basis he answered emphatically…Absolutely! He then asked if we would like to come by his place at some point in time where he could show us some really cool stuff he had found. Now don't get me wrong we were not afraid of this guy. He seemed very down to earth and normal. But this whole affair about Bigfoot and pictures was a little more than strange.

At any rate we exchanged numbers saying that it was nice to meet you and everything else in that regard. And we wrapped up the afternoons barbecue. Well let me tell you that for weeks after this meeting of Charlie. My wife and I had endless discussions about what we had seen and were told. Which brought us at some point to calling Charlie and arranging to see everything else that he said he had. When we had finally made it over to his house he had a really nice pad. The décor screamed of someone who loves the outdoors. There was woodsy and nature related stuff everywhere. Antlers on the wall. Rock collections in wooden trays. Photos of birds and animals and fish. And on one section of the wall there were about 20 photos of Bigfoot. We stood there looking at them as he told us in great detail about each photo and where he was when he took them. He then pointed out one in particular and said to us. Do you see this picture here? I was less than 20 feet away from this Bigfoot peeking over a log when I took this picture. We stood that close to each other for over 10 minutes before it walked away.

He then offered us something to drink and eat and told us to hang for a minute because he had some other things which he wanted to show us. He stepped into another room and returned with a sturdy wooden old milk bottle crate. He placed it gently on the table and started to carefully lift out of the crate some items which were wrapped in burlap. As he began to unwrap them placing them carefully around on the table top. They were plaster casts of footprints. Casts which he went on to tell us that had been gathered from many of his choice locations. He showed us the first one that he had ever found cradling it in his arms like it was a baby. But as he went on we found out that he no longer makes any casts. Because as he told us if I keep making them I will have no place to live. That's how many footprints he comes across now. He told us that he is so tuned in to where this group lives now that finding their footprints would be like your wife picking up your socks from around the house. We could clearly see as he showed us the individual prints. And as we now held them in our hands. That there were large ones and small ones. In other words children and adults in human terms. He referred to them as a clan of Bigfoot.

I will get back to this in a moment but there is something that I must interject with at this time. Later on my husband and I were both in total agreement about one single point. Why would a guy whose house was filled with so many beautiful natural artifacts. Have fake photos and staged footprints as part of his collection. It wouldn't make sense for him or anyone else to do so. In our opinion these items and photos were real. He took the photos and had found the footprints just as he had said. He saw we were more than interested and said the following to us. I want you to know that I have never taken anyone into this area before. But if you are game

I will invite you to come with me if you would like to. I told him that I would love to after which Sarah immediately interjected that we would let him know. Charlie just smiled. Happy wife happy life. Later on in the week having had many discussions about whether to go or not to go with Charlie. My wife had agreed that I could go. But that she would not go herself under any circumstances saying that it was much too dangerous. Not knowing where you are going or what you are getting yourself into.

At any rate Charlie and I got together on a date and time and met up. I was really excited. Before we began our excursion he said the following. These creatures are very quiet and docile. We are entering their home and should act in kind. He said I can't guarantee you anything other than this. If you follow my lead and stick with me. I promise you that you will see Bigfoot for yourself. Charlie said that Rome wasn't built in a day and everything that I have discovered can't be seen or hiked to in a day either. But if you are willing to spend the time I would be glad to have you tag along. I just smiled and started walking. The region we were entering which he referred to as their home was actually about 50 square miles according to Charlie. Perhaps even more. It was some fairly rugged real estate. And yet over time I realized that it wasn't all rugged. For at times we would be walking through relatively level timber and fire trails. But we will get back to that as we move along with this series of hikes and events. We hiked for hours through some rocky crags and hillsides eventually breaking out into some tall pines. He stopped by one spot to examine some trees that were toppled together. They were leaning against each other forming somewhat of a tee pee.

Charlie was pointing out that these types of tree formations are some of the first indications that are needed when locating Bigfoot.

It was his belief that they were territorial markers and or signposts. This was something he had come to believe over time. He went on as we walked around this teepee to point out how the trees had been placed and had not fallen here. In fact some of these trees as he later pointed out had come from hundreds of yards away. Many of them being very long and extremely heavy. We also noticed on closer inspection that one of the trees was fairly new. Charlie said that this tree was not part of the stack the last time I came here. Which he said indicates that the Bigfoot are looking after this to make sure it remains in good shape. It was obvious that none of the trees had fallen right there against each other. There were no stumps. And for the most part the trees which were part of the structure were not the same as the surrounding trees. They were most definitely brought there and set in place in my opinion. But the question was and is by whom or what? There is no way that a crew of strong men ventured in here to play a hoax on nobody. Because that's exactly how many people come through here according to Charlie.

Let's press on Charlie said because there is something else that you have got to see. We hiked for about another 45 minutes when we came upon an old shack that had almost completely collapsed upon itself over time. As we got closer Charlie said that when he first found this shack he was still able to walk inside. But now it was impossible. All we could do was look through what was left of a window. The roof being almost entirely folded in. But we could still see what it was he had brought me here to look at. He pointed out that inside there were lots of branches heaped up and flattened in one end of the room. When he first came here he said that it was in much better condition. And even then he could tell that it hadn't been used in a while. He said that there was a huge pile of scat that was dried up over in the corner. Scat that looked like a human's only king size. I could still see the pile but it was now like a dust heap. He believed that the Bigfoot were actually sheltering here at some point in time. But obviously no longer. And that was yet another thing which he pointed out. In all the time he had spent and with all the sightings he had. This was the only time he had run across something that remotely looked like a home or den. We started to head back when Charlie said to keep the faith.

This is a marathon not a sprint. I have been in here well over 500 times and have spent countless hours. And all of that time spent just to come across some of the things you are now seeing and that I have showed you at my house. And there is much, much more to see and do. And who knows we may see something on the way back. As it turns out we saw and heard nothing on the return hike. Basically we had retraced the steps we had taken coming in. I said to Charlie that what we had seen that day was very interesting but that obviously I was hoping for more. Of course he agreed with me.

However he stood his ground that this was a battle of attrition. And without the expenditure of time and effort nothing would or could be gained. We parted ways with him telling me to let him know when I wanted to go out with him again. That night my wife was amazed when I told her what we had seen and done. The reality was however that she was unimpressed. Charlie and I having not encountered a Bigfoot. Nevertheless I had contacted Charlie about a month later and we were back on the trail once again. We hiked right back into the same zone we had been in the last time. So I knew he was really committed to this area. But today we were going to detour into what he called the choke point.

As we were hiking we began to enter a point where we were above somewhat of a miniature canyon. There were two steep hillsides which flanked each other. The hillsides formed what I will describe as an entrance and an exit. Both of these sides were sporadically covered with brush and pines which made it very difficult to see at times and at others very easy. It depended on where you were positioned and where you were looking. So we sat down in a fairy high location where we had a good view of what he called the ambush point. As we sat down Charlie said that we are going to be staying here for a while so get comfortable. We were talking and he began to tell me of how he found this location and why we were staying here. He said that on two different occasions several years apart. He had found a deer carcass not far from the ambush point. One was most of the skeleton of a dead deer. And on the other occasion he had found a deer that may have been killed just a couple of days prior. Looking at the first one he had found being just a skeleton. Charlie noticed that one of the front legs was snapped in half. When he found the second deer several years later. Not only could he see yet again that one leg was broken like the other. But he also now saw that the head was twisted around like a towel as he described it.

And both carcasses were in the same area close to this ambush point. His belief at that time was that these deer were being killed and eaten near here because they had been ambushed here. As we were sitting and talking we were interrupted by a loud and clear audible wood knock. There was no doubt about it. This was wood on wood and as clear as day to the ears. Just one clean knock with nothing else following. And so we sat and sat and sat. Three hours later having seen and heard nothing more we left. Once we were well clear of the zone as he calls it. We began talking about the knock as well as the ambush spot. His opinion was that the knock was either a signal that we had been recognized. Or that a Bigfoot was signaling others of its position. He said that he never knocks back. He only waits quietly to see what develops after the knock has occurred. It was during one of these waiting sessions following a knock two years ago. That not one but three Bigfoot entered this small canyon. His view sitting on that day was that of what became known as the ambush point. Not knowing at the time that out of his view on the other end or entryway as he now refers to it. There were two more Bigfoot.

He said that this was actually a deer trail. But because the population was well dispersed he had only seen a few walking in here through the years. His theory being that the Bigfoot in the daytime somehow can plan on certain days that the deer will be coming through. It was just a theory and he had no way of proving it. To which I said to myself that you have to start somewhere and this was as good a theory as any in my opinion. On that day he watched as the small group which was comprised of several different size creatures including one monster as he called it. Began hiding and crouching behind some brush and boulders. He said that what transpired next had actually taken about an hour to develop. A doe had entered into his field of view. Apparently having walked in from the side he could not see. When suddenly the deer bolted being followed close behind by two other Bigfoot which were running in hot pursuit. The deer having nowhere to go ran squarely into where the others were lying in wait. It was then that one of the Bigfoot grabbed its limb knocking it to the ground and killing it with what appeared to be a twist of the head thereby breaking the creature's neck. This became the proof of what he had thought after finding the carcasses.

It was in fact the way that these Bigfoot were dispatching their prey. A broken leg and a broken neck. Charlie also developed another theory which was this. He had found many of what he called blinds in the woods. Which he said we would take a look at down the road sometime. He felt that during the day they would individually use a blind to conceal themselves by trails. Or they would act as a group by different choke points such as this little canyon. At night he felt that they could well enough conceal themselves being dark in color virtually anywhere. Although he personally never comes in here at night. All of his sightings and photos having occurred during daylight hours only. I have to tell you that I was really becoming a believer. When someone is on the cutting edge of something there will always be doubters and naysayers. But he had proof and quite a bit of it. I having now seen much of it with my own eyes. And having added to all of that this very day a knock. And now for your sake I will do a little fast forwarding or we will be here for days. Over the next 8 or 9 months I had been basically going out with him one day a month. He had taken me to see some of the blinds which were really impressive. They had been constructed just like a duck blind. Being put together with boughs from pines as shielding. With some sturdier branches having been used for support. All of them being in close proximity to well used trails. Looking at them one could clearly see that they had been constructed and not arbitrarily formed by any natural means.

Charlie was insistent that he had never heard so much as a single gunshot while in here. I had also seen with my very own eyes numerous prints which gave full credence to him saying that he doesn't make casts of them anymore. In the 9 months we were together I could have taken dozens of them myself. It was in I believe the tail end of month 9 that we were once again positioned to observe the choke or ambush point. When suddenly walking across the slope on the other side appeared a tremendous Bigfoot. Charlie turned to look at me with his eyes wide open and we both looked back at the creature. We had seen it walking for about 50 feet before it was once again concealed by trees. At no point did it turn or indicate that it had known or cared about us being there. Later on Charlie said that he believes they always know that we are there. His opinion being that of don't bother me and I won't bother you. He called this Bigfoot Big Daddy. He said we had just seen the largest of the clan. When I tell you that this thing was enormous. The available verbiage is not adequate. It had to have been 12 feet tall and the proportions of its body were such as nothing you can or could imagine. The utter thickness of its entire frame was incredible. If you have ever seen a movie of a large grizzly standing on its hind legs to look around in a field. This thing made that grizzly look like it was junior sized. And as big as it was its feet looked too big for its body. Now I wear a size 13. Well picture me walking in one day wearing a size 25 wide. They appeared that disproportionate to me. It looked like it was wearing clown shoes.

It was completely covered in reddish dark brown covered fur. And what would be its upper trap muscles seemed to hug its ear area. From the side it looked as though the head was tucked into the upper body somehow. It had a very lethargic and deliberate stride and arm swing which appeared as slow motion. Like it was gliding not walking. But I realized that it had covered some 50 feet in maybe 7 or 8 steps. Watching this thing was almost like an out of body experience which I can't really describe. It was as if a feeling or something had taken hold of me while it was there. I know that sounds weird and everything else but that's the best that I can do to describe what I was feeling at the time. It was an extremely odd experience to say the least. After it had passed Charlie clenched his fist while mouthing…Yes! That afternoon Charlie came home with me. He wanted to be there to see my wife's reaction when I told her what had happened today. Up to this point in time she was very stand offish about the whole affair. Well when she saw us come in together her immediate reaction was that of what happened? She was so happy for me. She knew that this had become a big deal for me personally. And now I had become the newest member of the Bigfoot sighting club. It was absolutely incredible.

✗

The Troopers Tale

The following story was brought to my attention by Gary Adair. Who at the time of this event was a trooper in the Northeast. I think that you will find it very interesting what he encountered while pursuing something entirely different. Well it's like I told you briefly when we first spoke. Dispatch had sent out a call asking all available units to report on the double to the scene of a domestic dispute. It was a woman calling for help saying that her husband was going to kill her with a sword. Now any type of law enforcement officer will tell you that these are the worst types of calls to go on. Many officers nationwide have been shot trying to diffuse such occurrences.

I was on my way as well as two other units as soon as the call came over the radio. As I arrived at the location which was a house trailer located deep into a wooded lot. Car 605 was ahead of me. We got out of the cars and went to the door with guns drawn. We could hear that there was quite a heated dispute still going on inside of the home. Including allot of cursing and yelling coming from a man and a woman. My partner pounded on the door shouting police. While I watched standing off to one end of the trailer home.

Just after he had knocked the female voice shouted… Good their here! And now you're going to jail you low life creep! Seconds after this as I was standing at the end of the trailer I heard a crash from the backside of the home. Which was followed by a man running out into a field wearing nothing but a pair of shorts and sneakers. He had forced his way out jumping through a window. I shouted to my partner that we have a runner which means someone trying to flee. I started in pursuit of the man as a third unit was just arriving. This unit upon seeing me giving chase to the man. Started running out into the field with his Bronco in pursuit of the same. The time was about 4 p.m. in the afternoon when the pursuit began. We heard over the radio that he didn't have a gun. And I had just stumbled and fell. Shortly after my taking a tumble and having gotten back to my feet the Bronco had reached a deep furrow that the truck could not cross. So now that officer and myself were both on foot chasing after this guy. The runner having already reached and entered into a wood line. Additional backup was already on the way as the two of us joined forces together entering into the tree line by ourselves.

We spaced ourselves about 40 yards apart and started walking in. Now a running man up here going into a desolate forest wearing only a pair of shorts is not going to last very long. I must have been several hundred yards into the forest when I came across a creek. I radioed to my partner about the creek being found. There was a slight embankment to it comprised of some moist brown soil which of course looked drier as you moved away from the water. After I told my partner about the creek he moved forward coming across it himself. This officer was going to move easterly looking for tracks of the man having crossed the creek and I was going to follow behind him. Both of us believing he had gone more in my partner's direction. As my partner was walking in one direction I was now heading in the same direction being about 50 yards behind him. The two of us looking for the man's tracks in the wet creek bed in order to determine where and if he had crossed it. As I was closing the gap between where I had started and where my partner had begun. I came across some gigantic impressions by the creeks edge. So close was I to whatever had made these that the impressions were still filling with water from the wet soil. One of them looked to be 2 or even 3 feet deep where the maker had sunk in very far. And the two prints which I initially saw had to have been close to 2 feet long and very wide. I radioed my partner to back track immediately to my position.

We both stood there examining the tracks. We could see one more print just on the other side of the creek as well. Which indicated that something had crossed the creek here. Now just so you can visualize this. The creek was maybe at its deepest point a foot. And it was maybe 12 feet wide in total including several feet on each side of bank or edging. There is no way that these tracks were those of the man we were chasing. We both walked through the water into the woods in the direction of the tracks. It was then maybe 40 feet into the woods on the other side that we found a sneaker. At this point there was no reason for the two of us to go on any further alone. We were on the radio the entire time and headed back out.

A man running scared and facing jail time can do strange things when trying to escape the law. So we retreated back to the field and the trailer. Reinforcements having already arrived I presented the sneaker to the wife who confirmed it was in fact her husbands.

Our office with the assistance of another agency began a manhunt. We staked out the various roads and areas where the man would eventually have to emerge. He couldn't last long with no clothing and one sneaker. After several days the man had not been seen or taken into custody. And the wife said that she hadn't seen him on or near the property. Neither had she or any relatives heard from him. During this time frame the giant impressions by the creek had obviously been the topic of much discussion. Them and the found sneaker as well. Some felt that they had been enlarged by the nature and softness of the creeks edge. Even after I had insisted they were not having seen then virtually within moments of them having been made. The water still trickling in as I told you earlier. This event after the passage of some two years' time had become a missing person case. The man still not being seen or found in all of that time. It was three or so years later that some hunters came across human skeletal remains about 5 miles north of where the chase had begun. They were hunting in some thick timber and had found them in a patch of tangled briars. After having been reported the remains were retrieved and brought in by our forensics people assisted by the hunters who brought them to their location.

After much examination of the remains and discussion as to who the skeleton belonged to. The missing man had become a suspect. DNA had been retrieved from the remaining spouse's child. The two having had the child together which turned up as being a match. The skeleton was in fact that of the runaway man from some three years earlier. But here is the real clincher of the story and why I had called you in the first place. The man's skull which was recovered had been caved in past the mid sagittal line according to the coroner. In other words the head had been smashed in more than half way. By what the coroner had said was a blunt force trauma. Now just to give you an idea of this type of force. If I was to take a full swing at your head with a large baseball bat. I couldn't even come close to this type of impact on your skull. Maybe not even with 2 or even 3 repeated forceful blows. And numerous of the skeletons ribs had been broken via compound fractures. These are clean fractures in which the bones are now broken into two pieces. All of this occurring while the man was apparently in the forest running and alone. It seems to me my dear readers. That something else had delivered the justice due to this violent man having escaped the long arm of the law. You live by the sword and you die by the sword. Your thoughts?

✗

No Bull

This report came to me from a retired executive living in western Kentucky. Here is Tim Hedges story. I had moved many years ago to the town in which I now live as part of an upward move within the company in which I was employed. A major shipping firm who's offices are located in Kentucky. It was in and through a local Masonic Lodge that I became acquainted with a group of men who were starting to form what they were calling a cattle consortium. I expressed some interest in learning about what their plans were as well as what would be involved in becoming a partner.

After a number of meetings and discussions. Each of the four starting members would be required to put up 250k for a total of 1 million dollars startup capital. We were going to begin raising Black Angus cattle for the retail food market. Now there is so much involved here that I could talk about. But suffice to say we were partnering with some farmers to make use of their pastures and fields in the form of a lease. Using their unused properties to raise our cattle on. It was quite an enterprise to get started but once all of the dots were connected we started on the road to profitability rather quickly.

My thoughts were that all of these guys myself included had a fair amount of business savvy. And even if we hadn't achieved success we could have literally sold off our stock with no problem whatsoever. The market being for Black Angus exceptional in nature. I had cashed out much of my corporate stock to fund my end of the venture. At that time in my life I was about 6 years away from my projected retirement and thought this would be a great future investment. Which as it turns out it was. This story actually began a year into my retirement or 7 years later. One of the ranchers whose farm we were leasing had begun to show a few losses of our Angus cattle. It started as some calves coming up missing. Some of which were found in the woods being badly mauled and partially eaten. As time went on other larger cattle were being found in the pastures with enormous wounds and flesh torn out of their hides. Having heard from the rancher and gone out to his farm on several occasions. We had all well surveyed the damage being done to the livestock.

It was the general disposition that a bear or perhaps even a cougar was the culprit. And that it would have to be shot to stop the mayhem. The farmer decided to hire a local hunter to both stake out and protect the herd. The herd on this farm alone at the time represented over 2 million dollars. And when you lose one of these beasts to a predator it represents a big hit to the pocket both now and into the future. Some having cost us a small fortune as breeding stock. Now it's not like these incidents had occurred in a weeks' time. They had actually been observed over a period of many months. There were actually six incidents in total at the time. Two of which had resulted in a mutilation and death and the others in injury to a still living animal. This hired hand was patrolling the pastures on horseback making it virtually impossible for him to be everywhere at once. The property being very vast and the herds being dispersed throughout. And even after having hired this gentleman over the next several months one mature female and another calf had still been taken under his watch. Both being found in the woods having been partially eaten.

One of the oddities being that none of the fences had been taken down or damaged in any way. Which would indicate something having breached it. Whatever was doing this came over the fence and went back out over the fence carrying hundreds of pounds with it. With no apparent damage having been done to the fence in the process. To date all that the hand had seen was some bobcats and a couple of coyotes. None of which was capable of inflicting such carnage on the herd. It was on one night in the fall that the hand had planned to ride up until about midnight. Not that the time really mattered. But upon our request he was asked to mix up his shifts a bit in hopes of catching whatever was killing the cattle. On this day with the darkness falling a little sooner he was riding through one pasture and heading over to check on another herd.

When suddenly from behind him he heard an uproar from the herd he had left some 10 minutes earlier. Turning his horse about and galloping back he was shocked as he came over the hill to find the herd huddled in one end of the pasture. He immediately began to survey the pasture when his eyes became fixed on a large mass out in the middle that was not moving. As he approached the mass in the darkness he now realized that he was looking at the bull lying on the grass. He began to circle it when his horse began to buck not being willing to continue in the area. So he dismounted to discover the grim reason behind the bulls lying there. Its head had been torn from its body. And the same head was nowhere to be seen. It was in fact gone. He went back to the house to tell the owner of his discovery. They took the pickup truck and a flood light and headed back out into the pasture together. When they got up on the scene with the trucks lights on and the flood lamp illuminating it. What they saw was incredible to say the least. The bulls head had been torn from the shoulders including the spinal column. I mean it was ripped off not severed. This as it were was a major blow. For the most important animal in the pasture was this strong viable bull. It was in and through his prowess that the herd itself remained viable and growing. And what could tear the head off a bull was beyond our comprehension.

He was worth his weight in gold and now he was dead. A decision had to be made and soon as to just how we were going to deal with this dilemma moving forward. The losses to date were mounting into the tens of thousands of dollars with no end in sight. Either whatever was doing this was going to be killed or we would abandon this pastureland and move our herds elsewhere. So a plan was devised to stake out the acreage with as many armed men as was thought needed to kill the beast that was attacking the herd. In the end we had hired 13 men. Each was to be stationed in a different area and all would be in contact via radio. We were now fully committed to killing this monstrosity. Of the 13 men 7 had night vision sights on their guns. This pastureland was staked out for 3 weeks without a single event occurring after the death of the bull. It was on the 23rd night of our 24 hour stake outs that one of the men over the radio reported something running across the pasture on all fours that looked like a massive bear. Moments later he was heard saying… Oh my God! It's standing on two legs now and walking toward the herd. It's gigantic! Seconds later the sound of two rifle shots broke the silence of the night. He started shouting…I got it! I got it! Everyone started to converge on that end of the pasture when the hunter started shouting into the radio that it was running towards the fence line. The search continued throughout the night for whatever he had shot and nothing had been found.

He swore up and down that it was moving quickly across the pasture on all fours when suddenly it stood on both legs and started walking. He said he could see it clearly in the night vision scope. It was some type of massive furry beast walking like man having run most of the pasture like a bear. He said that when it was on its feet nearing the herd he could see that it was at least twice the height of the cattle's backs. All the men having given it their all in the search had stopped looking. The police had been called and nothing was found until two days later. It was then on the local news that a report was blurted out of a motorist having seen what she described as a dead Bigfoot on the side of the highway. We had made calls to the police department after hearing of the report and they denied there being any Bigfoot found. They said what she had seen was a dead black bear and nothing more. Well as it turns out. After our man put two rounds in the giant hairy beast that night. And after the woman said she saw a dead Bigfoot on the roadside followed by the police denying it whole heartedly. Our problem had ended rather abruptly. Not a single head of cattle was ever injured or found dead in that pastureland again from that point in time forward.

X

The South Carolina Incident

The following report came to my attention via Steven Wellesley. A resident of South Carolina who apparently came into a large inheritance. And something else that was rather large to go along with it. Here is Stevens account.

My mother had passed away several years ago this past June. I was the only child my brother having been killed in the Desert Storm campaign. My inheritance among other things was my mother's home and property in the northern section of South Carolina. It consisted of a large old plantation home nestled in about 90 acres of land. The land way back in the day was used for growing cotton but hadn't seen any of that for close to a hundred years. My brother and I had grown up on this land hunting and fishing and the like in the surrounding area. My father having died about 12 years before my mother's passing it had been just me and my mother for quite some time. Now my wife and I didn't live far from my mother's place. Our two children were grown and had their own lives. It was then that she and I had decided to live in my parents' home and rent our own house out. The house was beautiful and grand in scale. The previous owner as well as the family who built it we very well to do. The woodworking and attention to detail throughout the home was top notch and had been maintained by my father until his passing. He was a man that treated this house like the curator of a museum would. The property consisted of about 90% grassland and the rest was woods.

There was also a small creek which ran through the northeast portion of the property. The grass which my father used to cut with an old Farm All tractor had been growing wild since his passing. And out in the fields there were 14 different fruit trees which were very old as trees go. Peach, apple and cherry to be exact. I remember my mom baking delicious pies and tarts as a youth. And she had a place in our pantry for all the preserves and jams that she would make. You wouldn't dare walk out in that grass now because in its current state I am sure it was chock full of snakes. At some point I had re-fired the old tractor and began to cut the fields back into shape again. It's funny looking back now having lived in the house myself for a while. But I had never noticed that with all of the details in keeping the house original. The back door had been replaced with a steel door at some time.

I don't know if it was done when my dad was alive. Or if my mother had it replaced while she was here alone at some point. But neither of them had ever mentioned it and I had never noticed it. I only mention it because a steel door being installed on this house was really odd. There was one large barn out back where my dad kept the tractor and some yard tools. But other than that is was basically empty space inhabited by some barn owls. When I realized that the owls were in there living I always left the doors slightly open for them. It was really cool to watch them going in and out. We had been there for almost two years and everything was working out perfectly. I was feeling like I was a child again reliving my youth on the land and in the house which I had grown up in. It was in the summer and fall of our second year that as I look back things started getting a little weird on the property. My wife and I had started hearing some loud howling emanating from off in the distance. Way back in the far end of our land or beyond. It would always begin around dusk. And there were many nights when we could hear it in the middle of the night waking us from our sleep. It was a long steady howling noise very much like a fire departments siren in both volume and its duration. But much deeper in sound.

I never really remember saying anything to my wife other than it was some animal in the woods. But I didn't recall any such sounds being present there while growing up. Now as I said earlier I had been cutting the fields. And because of this my wife and I now had gained access to the fruit trees once again. And this was their season for yielding fruit. Don't get me wrong we weren't like my mom making preserves and pies or anything like that. But we were picking some of the fruits as they ripened to eat. When I tell you that I am not a farmer that would be an understatement. But I started to notice that the fruits on the trees were disappearing. My wife and I were picking maybe a couple of dozen pieces a week. Which wasn't even a smidgeon of what was there for the picking. I wasn't even pruning them and each tree had to have been producing a thousand pieces of fruit.

And the cherry trees output was incredible. I mean bushels and bushels of fruit. When I was young my mother and father were grabbing almost every piece that the insects or birds didn't damage. And the rest would fall to the ground and rot. What I was seeing was quite the contrary. Fruit was disappearing from the trees. And virtually nothing was being left on the ground. I mean it was basically just scraps or remnants of the fruit which was left lying around.

These trees were being stripped of their fruit as fast as it ripened. And for the life of me I couldn't wrap my head around who or what may be doing this. I had told my wife and she just lifted her hands as if to say whatever. It was after the fall had changed to winter. And the trees had long since stopped yielding any more fruit. When my wife was in the kitchen one night preparing our dinner. That I heard what sounded like a pot falling into the sink as my wife exclaimed. Oh my gosh! A shout which was followed by her running into the den. She was visibly shaking and as white as a ghost as she sat down in the chair holding her head in her hands. I said to her honey what's wrong? She didn't answer me. I asked her again what happened to you? She looked at me as she was kind of gathering her composure. I was washing the dishes not really paying attention to anything in particular facing the window over the sink. And as I lifted my head to put a clean pot into the dishrack the most hideous face that you could imagine was looking at me through the window. And as quick as I saw it the face was gone. Honey you have to call the police right away. I'm not kidding. Whatever that was is out there in our yard right now. So I picked up the phone and made the call. I told them that there was a prowler in our yard that my wife had seen looking in our window.

They said that an officer would be right over. The officer arrived and we watched him pull in. Opening the door we stepped out to greet him as my wife started to frantically tell him what had happened to her. He told her to try and calm down and asked her to show him the window she had seen the prowler from. I could tell he was trying to see if there was anything that could have made a reflection looking like a man in the glass. And that's when my wife said to him. It wasn't a man. It was the face of a ghoul. It was horrible beyond description. I could see it in his face that he was wondering what kind of people we were with my wife talking about a ghoul. She started to describe to him what happened. Telling him that it had wideset eyes that were much larger than ours. And she said that it was smiling with what she said was the most demonic grin she had ever seen. The width of the grin being something like eight inches or more. And as soon as she had locked eyes with it the thing was gone from sight. The officer said that he was going to go outside and have a look around. I told him you can go out right here. It was then that I thought about the steel door which we were now going out of. I walked outside with him carrying a fire poker in my hand. He had a really big Maglite that was in his belt loop. And as he began shining it around he put the beam right on the barn doors. The doors were open. But before I could say anything he asked me if I always leave my barn open.

I told him that the one door on the right is always open a crack for the barn owls to go in and out. But when I came inside before those doors were not open like that. So the two of us walked over to have a look see. I am telling you flat out. God as my witness. The hair was standing up on the back of my head as we walked towards the barn. I felt as though something was breathing down my neck.

As he put the light into the barn and shone it around there was nothing inside. Nothing except the tractor and the tools used for around the house. He asked me if I could see anything missing to which I said no. We kept walking around the house shining the light here and there and saw absolutely nothing. But I had the creepiest feeling that we were being watched as he and I went back into the house. He began speaking looking us squarely in the eyes. I am not about to say that you didn't see anything because I can see that you are obviously still shook up over this. The doors were open on your barn which you said were closed. Maybe there was some local hoodlum prowling around looking to walk off with something they could sell. It was then that my wife broke in hysterically saying it was not man. It was some kind of monster!

He said I understand. But there is really nothing more I can do here tonight. Why don't you leave all the lights on and stay up until you have calmed down? Have a glass of wine and try to compose yourself. Whoever or whatever this was has gone off. If anything else should happen just call the station and we will be right over. My wife was beside herself as the officer said goodbye and left. She said to me Honey I cannot and will not stay here. I was trying to console her by saying that whatever she saw was just passing through and had evidently moved on not finding anything of interest. Oh yeah she said. What about those darn fruit trees being picked clean. Maybe it was this same demon from hell eating our fruit. And how about this. Has it dawned on you that maybe your mother had this steel door installed for protection? I'd be willing to bet that she had seen something and didn't want to bother us over it. You know how she was being all stubborn and everything. She probably saw that monster through the kitchen window just like I did.

At that point in time I really couldn't and didn't want to get into a debate with her. And as I already told you my hair was standing on end when I was walking around with the police officer. Something really didn't feel right out there. And when I saw those barns doors opened wide and new that something was wandering around my house while my wife and I were inside relaxing. That can most definitely make one feel a little uneasy inside. As it turns out we both fell asleep that night sitting in the living room. When morning had come and I was up and about I went outside to have a look around. Everything that seemed so eerie during the night had changed dramatically with the coming of a new day. I didn't see anything unusual around the property and I actually fired up the tractor to take a ride around the land. I was thinking of my father who loved to cut the fields driving around in any kind of weather. It was great therapy for me especially after the night we had. Later that morning my wife and I took a little ride into town to get a few things. When we were leaving the store there was a small newspaper rack on the way out that was always there. The paper being a local gazette that was free of charge.

But today a certain headline on the front pages lower right side caught my attention. It read as follows. Booger Sighted by Woman on Highway. I quickly folded up a copy without mentioning why to my wife. Later that day while my wife was showering I pulled out the paper to read the article. It said that a local woman had sighted a Bigfoot walking down the shoulder of a highway. And her sighting was the day before my wife said she saw a ghoul in the kitchen window. The area of the highway where the woman said that she had seen it was only a few miles from our property. The fact of the matter was that if I was to take a walk way up through my land and cut across the woods instead of taking the long way around using the roads. It was more than likely about a mile from our house as the crow flies.

It was the very night that I had read the article that I heard the howling again while my wife was sleeping. I was now convinced in my heart that my wife had seen the same beast the woman had seen on the highway. And that the source of this howling was one in the same. I was also becoming more certain that my wife may be correct about the door change on the house. What else could be the reason for swapping out a beautiful old undamaged door on the house? A door that more than likely would have been around for another 200 years had it not been replaced. I was also now convinced that this thing was responsible for eating the fruit off the trees in our fields. I think it was maybe 3 or 4 days after this night of which I just spoke. That during the day I went for a long walk out into the field behind our home. I was really troubled inside as to what to do. Now I had become the one who was concerned about this beast. I was strolling slowly kind of kicking the grass and looking at the sky as I did so. And I was thinking about my wife and my parents. I was reaching a point in the field where having walked up an incline for a couple of hundred yards the back section of the property could now be seen. From the house you could only see this portion of the land from the third story windows. My head had just broken above the plane where I could now see this area. It was then that coming into view I could see a large black creature walking along the edge of the field. I ducked down just enough to allow my eyes to continue watching it without being seen myself. Even at the distance I was watching from I could easily gauge the enormity of this thing.

I could use every adjective imaginable to describe it. Tall, big, thick, muscular, hairy and damn near anything else you can think of. It slowly covered about 2 acres of land and disappeared into the woods. I went back to the house without saying a word to my wife. Who by the way knows now everything that I had seen that day but she didn't then. I casually brought up the sale of the house. The house being more than we really needed at this stage of our lives. And my attachment for the old house which we were now renting to tenants. She was not against my decision to sell. Whatever you want to do is fine with me. I just don't want to see that ghoulish face anymore. And so our saga ended. The house was sold and we moved into another rental house until our tenants lease was up. I asked Steven to add any details of what he had seen even though the distance was great. Here is what he said. First of all there is nothing that can prepare you for this type of thing. It is instantaneously a sensory overload. I had seen a large buck down at that end of the property once and it was barely visible. And this thing stood out clearly. I could see the sun shining on its fur.

It was very tall and I couldn't even venture a guess as to how tall. It looked like a black block of living creature walking along. Its arms were extremely long and swung in a slow cadence with each of the steps it took. The movements being very deliberate. It moved like it was the king and it knew it. I don't believe that it has any competition in the woods. And I am certain having seen it for myself that it could make short work of anything or anyone that got in its way. There is one other thing that I would like to mention about this whole affair. My uncle used to live some 6 miles from a busy train station in Atlanta. If you were outside during the morning commute time. When that train was leaving the station it would sound its horn. And when I was at my uncle's house I could hear it 6 miles away. Now let me say this. This Bigfoots howl was so loud and resounding. That I am sure people can hear it for miles around. And yet to a person I have never heard a single soul speak of hearing it. And these things are being reported all over the place including now on my parents old farm. I don't know if people are afraid to speak of it or what. But it has to be being heard in many other places and by many other people. Well my dear readers. I cannot even begin to comprehend looking through my kitchen window and seeing a Bigfoot staring back at me. What about you?

✗

The Roosevelt Elk Encounter

This account was given to me by Edwin Wright and his hunting partner George Hendrickson. Both of whom are residents and hunters from the state of Oregon. Here is their story. Each year Georgie and I plan a week of fall hunting in Washington's rainforest. This year's hunt was for Roosevelt Elk which can only be found in a few areas of the world. The coastal mountain range of Washington State being one of those locations where they live and thrive. In this region the elk live in the thick, dense underbrush and forest. The logging country of the Pacific Northwest seems to be a preferred habitat for these creatures as well. This region of the United States receives well over 100 inches of rainfall annually and because of this the underbrush is extremely lush. Now any hunter will tell you that this thick underbrush brings with it advantages and disadvantages. The advantages being that of plenty of cover for the hunter as well as being an ideal habitat for the animals. The disadvantages being the constant rain and dampness. And the extremely limited visibility for taking a quality shot at your prey. Most rifle shots will be taken at a range of 75 yards or less and your typical bow shot is between 20 and 30 yards. With one of my own being taken at 5 yards. That's how close you can get in these forests to the animals.

It is because of the diverse weather and habitat challenges that are presented to the hunter where the Roosevelts live. That they are one of the most difficult species to hunt. Eddie is totally correct in what he just told you. And it is because of this difficulty that time spent on the hunt has a direct correlation to your success rate. Eddie and I keep a detailed hunting log on each of our trips. By doing so we can fine tune our techniques over time to ensure successful hunts as we move into the future. We have found that when we plan hunts for 10 to 12 days we have a 100% success rate. With a 5 day hunt yielding between say 60 and 80% success. Our typical hunt consists of using both bow and rifle. We start with the bow being our preferred method and if we find ourselves coming down to the proverbial wire with the amount of time we have left in our trip. The rifle becomes our weapon of choice. There are so many times when the animal is so close and yet so far for an effective bow shot in this undergrowth. Whereas the rifle can be effective on day one for the well-schooled hunter.

What George just said is totally true in every sense of the word. So if you are going to have success with the bow all of your ducks must be in order. And that starts with technique and location. Our most successful methodology to date is still hunting within the confines of a well timbered canyon. That and or being near any river drainage areas that you can find. We also will construct blinds in well-travelled areas using calls to attract bulls. Getting real aggressive with them when they start to get in tight to our position. The two of us generally like to situate ourselves near to each other whenever possible. The slope of a canyon being our preferred haunt. It is from this position that we have had the greatest success in sighting moving animals both above and below our position. Of course having done everything right with blind setups and everything else. An elk can surprise you by moving right across your path while you're stalking being taken down with a quick shot. Whenever possible we will bring our quad in the truck. We do this to try and get as close as we can to our area before the hiking begins. It's also a great help in taking the meat out when we get lucky. For this particular hunt we had planned for 4 days. Even though this is on the lowest end of the success window. We knew the area extremely well where we were going and our confidence level was very high.

We had good success there in the past and we felt that we would score again. After setting up our tent by the truck we took the quad into the forest and began our days hunt. It's a rough hike into this terrain but the two of us workout hot and heavy during the year to prepare ourselves for such excursions. The area we were heading into was a steeply sloped canyon that had a very well used trail running up and down within it. The trick in here was not that of seeing animals but rather the ability to position yourself in the best possible way to get off a quality bow shot. So many times an elk was just out of effective range or had slipped behind some cover right as you were ready to let go with a broad head. And that my friend is hunting. Day one had come and gone with no Roosevelts being seen. On day two we headed directly back into the same location being satisfied with what we had seen the day before as far as overall animal population goes. This day we had seen a giant 5 x 5 Roosevelt bull walking by us at about 50 yards. We waited and waited for him to come closer but no such luck. We had also seen a 3 x 3 after him but passed in hopes of the larger more mature bull.

Typically when hunting and in particular if you have a guide. They will always advise the fare to take what you can when you can because you may not get another opportunity. This is in fact the best course of action for most hunters especially if you don't hunt that frequently. But we hunt quite frequently and have an experience level that is more than likely higher than most others. And it because of this that we were determined to get the 5 x 5 or perhaps even better. The next day we had gone in and moved our makeshift blinds to a slightly lower position. This would allow this bull should he come in again to be marginally closer to us than the day before. The big question being would he come back again? So we positioned ourselves and began the wait. It was 11:17 in the morning when what must have been about 30 elk came running down the trail. I know the time because I had just looked at my watch. You never see these animals running unless they have been frightened. We both looked at each other across the opening in the brush between the two blinds. It was exactly at 11: 21 just four minutes after the herd had run through when I heard the snap of a branch and my eyes rolled to the left in the direction of the sound.

Passing behind an opening in some pine boughs I could see a tremendous black figure moving down the trail. I gave a small finger signal to Georgie and a moment later a gigantic Bigfoot appeared walking through a break in the trees where the herd had just run by. Three steps later he was once again concealed by the pines. And then he reappeared having passed by the cover yet again. We watched him as he walked down the entire trail toward the base of the canyon. Coming in and out of our view numerous times before walking out of our sight completely. The two of us came out of our blinds speechless. Looking at each other and down into the canyon in the direction where he had walked. It was as though for a few moments in time we were unable to put any words together. I was completely and totally dumfounded by what had just transpired. Finally I said to ED something like did that just really happen? I don't know if you remember Ed but you just stood there. You didn't even answer me. I know I was in a complete and utter daze. I guess it was as close to a state of shock as I will ever come. It was as if my mind had short circuited. I couldn't think or act or say anything. I was momentarily shut off as a human being. I'm surprised I didn't crap in my pants or something. I'm not even sure if it had come towards us I could have pulled my rifle out and shot. I felt like I was under some type of mind control as it came into view and passed by. It was like all of my abilities had been put on hold. It is very difficult to describe or put into words. I think it must have been about 15 or 20 minutes before we had regained full functionality. The forest had become completely still with no sign of life whatsoever being present. We walked over to the trail and there were no indications of any prints so to speak. Just wide flattened areas where it had walked. The ground being very hard and well-travelled with pine needles and debris on both sides of the trail.

The two of us had heard all of the talk of Bigfoot. We were living and hunting in places where most say that they have seen them. And yet we had seen nothing of the sort ourselves. That is to say until that day on the Roosevelt hunt. When the fog in our minds had dissipated we went back to the truck and tried to sort out for our notebook all of the details. Our sighting had occurred at about 11:20 a.m. It was drizzling out and we had our rain gear on in the blinds. We had seen the elk herd run by followed by hearing the branch snapping. When it first came into view in hind sight the Bigfoot was not giving chase to the elk. It was just travelling and had more than likely spooked the herd. It must be seen as a predatory animal to them or they would not have run in such a fashion. It was much higher than us because of our position in the blinds. And at no time did it stop or turn to look in our direction. It seemed to be completely unaware of our presence. The two of us agreed that it had to be every bit of 8 to 10 feet tall. Just a tremendous monster of a beast. Neither one of us could remember measuring it up to anything it had either passed through or by. It was like a giant mega monster in a comic book or something. It reminded me of the way they depict the Hulk busting out of a shirt and flexing his muscles.

When it was relatively speaking passing in front of us we could see the dark brownish black fur. It was hanging off the body and looked kind of shaggy. Not at all like a bear's coat. It was like a long haired dog breed that was never brushed. I remember distinctly the hands being like 20 inches long. They were just massive hands like an oversized baseball mitt. Its head and shoulders looked like one piece. There was no neck visible as we know it. As it descended the slope heading down and away from us the upper torso was clearly in a V shape like that of a body builder. If I had to venture a guess as to the width I would say 5 feet or better across the shoulders. And here's another thing that comes to mind. From the back view the muscles of its upper back were so enormous. That at least half of the head which could be seen from the side was consumed in those muscles. Which also brings to mind the side profile. Its jaw line was clearly protruding forward from the rest of the face. While the nose appeared as though it was almost flush to the face. Ed is 100% right about that. Another thing was the color of its skin. I only recall seeing skin on the face and fingers. But what skin that I did see looked almost black or an extremely dark grey color at best. Its face also seemed deeply wrinkled like it had grooves in it instead of wrinkles. We actually left that day having not scored a kill and headed back to Oregon. I think I can say this for the both of us. We are different people today because of that event. We will never hunt or go into the woods with the same mindset that we once had. Seeing that Bigfoot had transformed our lives and our thinking about hunting and life in general.

✗

The Prairie Creek Redwoods State Park Sighting

This encounter really got my attention because I had myself walked through the very area where the encounter took place some 20 years ago. Here is Debbie Stillmans account of just what she saw when jogging during the month of August 2011. My girlfriend and I decided to spend the weekend in Elk Prairie Campground in California. Located right at the Prairie Creek Redwoods State Park in Orick. The two of us are avid runners so after breakfast we slipped on our sneaks and went out for a run. Our plan was to take the Cal Barrel to Rhododendron Trail which is just slightly over a 4 mile loop. And perhaps taking a cut off onto some secondary trails depending how the run went. As we began our jog I have to be honest with you that most of this area is extremely difficult to run in. The trails can be very narrow and tight. Running in-between large trees, hills, ferns and felled trees. So yes our intent was to run but at many points we were just fast walking and digging on the crazy scenery. The woods here is very mystical even during a bright beautiful day which it was. There are glimpses and glimmers of sunlight shimmering through the canopy of this magnificent old growth redwood forest. There are some really old hollowed out or tunneled trees in here. Which form open arches and tube like structures that just beckon you to walk through them. The two of us had more than a little fun climbing around and through them during our run. The trails in this park kind of wandering around through the woods. At times depending on the direction you are heading a ray of sunlight may be poking through which somewhat blinds you for a moment like a cars bright beams in the darkness of night.

Everywhere there are ferns and what appears to be a haze floating around within the trees. It's just really fantastic and like I said before mystical. We were well into our run having already veered off the trail onto a secondary fork. We had stopped to take a look around at the foliage surrounding this one area of the trail when my girlfriend said to me. What the heck is that? She was pointing at a large redwood off to our right. And I said to her what the heck is what? Because I didn't see anything. She said I just saw something duck behind that big tree over there. Right there I swear to you. So we both stood watching. As we watched for maybe two minutes. We saw what was the top of a head and one eye peering out from the side of the tree. It was a furry head of something like a gorilla or a large chimpanzee. As quickly as we had set eyes on it the creature ducked back behind the tree. I am talking maybe only 50 feet away from us. No sooner had we seen it when it jumped suddenly from being behind one tree to being behind the one next to it. It was a leap of well over 10 feet or more and it had performed this leap in one clean movement. So fast that if we weren't watching it directly I believe we would have missed it.

After seeing it jump we realized that this was no little monkey. It must have been crouching down when we first caught a glimpse of it. I say this because when it jumped not only did it completely leap from behind one tree to being completely behind the other. We could see that it was about 7 or 8 feet tall and really wide. My girlfriend Wendy put both of her hands against her mouth and said oh my God it's a Bigfoot! With that we turned and started walking quickly away in the same direction that we had just come from. I was somewhat looking over my shoulder while trying not to stumble or get hurt when I saw it dart into the woods in the direction we were now heading. It was on the other side of a fern covered mound that was to our right. Just so you can picture this and understand. There are so many parts of this forest where your visibility is very limited by a host of different things. Either by the enormous trees themselves. Huge trunks that are downed on the ground. The ferns and the brush which is everywhere. And this light and dark effect formed by the canopy over your head. We were walking fast and started to run as we were able to do so. I could hear this thing running in the woods next to us. It was flanking our movements and keeping pace with us. Once or twice I saw its body briefly flash by an opening in the underbrush.

My girlfriend was screaming now and saying that it's going to get us. God please help us! Please help us! She was shouting and crying as we ran. I was so frightened that tears were rolling down my cheeks and I couldn't stop them. We were getting whacked in the face with branches like whips. As we passed between some trees in this really tight snakelike turn my pinky finger caught an edge and broke clean out to the side of my hand with a snap. It was just hanging like the letter L off the side of my hand. We kept running.

As best as I could reckon we were at least 3 miles from camp and this monster was still pacing us. I could hear it puffing or grunting now and It couldn't have been more than 40 feet off to our side. I could hear branches snapping and whacking around as it ran. I grabbed my girlfriend and said you have to stop or you will have a heart attack. Her chest was pounding in and out from crying and running. She was hysterical. We can't stop it will kill us! I said to her if it wanted to kill us it would have done so already. I grabbed a log and gave it to her picking up another one for myself. I told her to try and calm down a little. We will keep walking fast and carry these as a weapon. There is no way that we can continue to outrun this thing. It's been right next to us for the past half mile or whatever it's been.

We kept walking fast and my girlfriend kept sobbing. I could still hear the Bigfoot cracking and smashing its way through the brush. And I couldn't help wondering why it wasn't exposing itself or charging us. Maybe this was some crazy game for it. After all it was hiding behind the trees when we first saw it. Why it could have rushed us right then and there and been done with it but it didn't. It was right as I was thinking this that I realized I couldn't hear it any more. After maybe another quarter mile or so I was convinced it was gone. I told my girlfriend to stop because it was gone. We stood there gasping and hugging each other telling each other it's alright. Everything's going to be fine. A little further on the trail opened up slightly where we could see much further in most directions. And the Bigfoot was nowhere to be seen. We said to each other that maybe it was just scaring us off. And if that was the case it had done its job and well. I asked Debbie to tell me all the details that she could remember from the few moments they had seen the creature and here is what she told me. When I first saw it I didn't know until later that I was only seeing a very small piece of its head and one black eyeball. And then it ducked back behind this huge redwood. At that time based on the height of what I had seen. I thought it was about 4 feet tall.

But when it jumped its height had doubled to maybe 7 or 8 feet. I don't mean to keep repeating myself. But the way it jumped in one clean bound or whatever you want to call it. Leaping from being completely behind the one tree to being completely behind the other tree. The area between the trees being at least 10 feet was absolutely incredible. I don't know anything that can do such a thing. It was then that we saw it fairly well. It was either a reddish blonde or a reddish grey in color. Suffice to say it was red and a somewhat lighter color in combination. The lighting was not very good from where we were and where it was. It had very long and muscular legs and arms. Just like all the pictures you have seen through the years. And its feet for the record were in fact big.

The funny thing was that I could see the hair hanging and kind of overlapping its feet when it was in the air. And briefly I saw that its back and rump was covered in all kinds of debris. The hair on the head was noticeably longer than the hair covering the rest of its body. But as far as I could see it was fully covered in fairly long hair everywhere that was in view. Again I am talking about 2 seconds in the air and that's it. Out of the corner of my eye as we began to run I had seen it again but just briefly. And from that angle I couldn't give you anything more than I have already told you. But this much I will say. I don't know how anything could run crashing through the brush like that thing did without being hurt badly. It was a nonstop run filled with cracking branches and trees. And why it didn't come out is beyond me. When we got back to camp I got a free ambulance ride to get my finger splinted after having reported to the rangers what had just happened on the trail. They were completely blown away by our report and we could see them going immediately into the trail after the ambulance was taking us out. And that's my story.

✗

The Dead Falls Lake Affair

I am going to warn you coming into this tale. That this may be the freakiest sighting that I have ever heard of. And it begins right now as Marion Lane and her brother Chris weave this amazing story. There was a group of us at the time perhaps close to 20 people. I don't recall exactly the number of persons. This was 1984 so it was quite a while back. Anyway we had planned to head into the Shasta National Forest hiking up to Dead Falls Lake and doing a little overnighter with the guitars and beers. It was July. If you've never been there Mount Eddy Lake and Dead Falls Lake pretty much sit in what I would call a bowl. They are virtually completely surrounded by mountain peaks.

There isn't much of a shoreline on the lake but rather an abrupt meeting of the surrounding hills and trees with the edge of the water. But it is a fantastic and desolate spot. And a great destination for those who are seeking such a place in particular at night. Our typical gig was to basically hike in and crash on a blanket when we couldn't stay up anymore. So the whole crew had made it in and began the night's festivities. It was turning out to be a pretty good night. We had some campfire singalongs.

Some hotdogs and oh yes the beers. It was about 2 a.m. when we first noticed a blue glowing illumination over one of the peaks to our north. It was really odd considering there isn't anything out here but people like us this hour of the night. This light I should also add was emanating from thousands of feet up and glowing over the peak. Needless to say it had all of our attention. Some were sitting and others were standing as we watched the blue light growing in intensity. It seemed as though whatever was the source of the light was about to come over the peak. And some ten minutes or so later there it was. Although it was miles away at the time we first saw it. We could now see it was a large glowing disk exuding what was a combination of blue and white extremely bright light. Which from a distance almost appeared like the disk was alive. I know this is really weird but you will know why I mention it in a minute. This thing really had our attention now as you could well imagine. As it slowly made its way over the peak it was very gradually making its way down into the valley. The valley in which we were gathered.

As it was beginning what was a descent beams of light started to emanate from different sides of the object. First from one side and then another. They were flashing on and off and appeared to be scouring the terrain like a search grid of some kind. Some of the group were already getting antsy and afraid. In particular the girls. But when I tell you that there was nowhere to run and hide I am not kidding. Particularly from something flying overhead with bright searchlights. It was getting closer and closer to our position and whatever it was could certainly see our blazing fire. So everyone started throwing dirt on it and squirting it with beer. Others were filling empty bottles with water from the lake to extinguish it. It was difficult to gauge the distance and size of this object. But it was slowly coming towards the lake and the entire landscape was glowing beneath it as these random searchlights kept flashing off and on in all directions. All of us could now see that the craft seemed to be somewhat organic. Basically it was glowing with a yellowish white color now. But swirling around within this base color was a bright blue. It looked like pigment when it is added to a can of paint as you start to mix it in with a stick. It was beyond your wildest imagination.

I would say that about ten minutes or so had passed. All of us being more than stunned by this spectacle. When about half of the group said that they were getting the heck out of here and the rest stayed. My thought was that the ones who run in the movies get attacked. But there was no stopping them. It think about 8 or 9 people left. This ship or craft was at the other end of the lake now which was still a considerable distance away. We could now see that the edge of the lake was being illuminated by the glow. By this time I could now say that this disk was at least 200 feet across and possibly a good deal more. And then all of a sudden it stopped and began to pulse. Brighter and dimmer. Brighter and dimmer. Very much like a heartbeat. All of the spot or searchlights had stopped. And a ring of fuzzy multi colored lights started to appear circling around its outer edge. They were red, green and yellow and they appeared to be very fuzzy and kind of unfocused. They weren't sharp beams like the searchlights. They just were kind of glowing and encircling the craft.

It sat there unmoving over this one spot for almost 20 minutes. When suddenly a wide beam of somewhat powder blue light flashed from its base to the ground below. To us it appeared as a column of light. A perfectly bordered and contained shaft or tube of blue light. Its origin being the central bottom section of the craft continuing right down to the ground. The craft continued to pulse while the shaft of light was on the ground. Our fire was completely out now and we were standing in the pitch dark in total awe of what we were seeing. At some point we all started saying that there was something being drawn up from the ground within this tube of light. From our vantage point it looked like a speck. But there was most definitely something that was now illuminated being pulled up or rising up within the shaft of light. Whatever that something was had stopped about midway between the ground and the craft. It was literally suspended in midair within the light.

Everything else stayed just as I described it to you for maybe another 10 or 15 minutes and nothing changed. It was then that several other specks started to descend from the crafts base moving downward in the tube of light. These specks were much smaller than the one that was suspended after being drawn up from the ground. Again from the distance we were there was no way of telling what any of these things were that were in the blue light shaft. They were simply specks in the distance. I could see these specks descending in the tube and stopping right where whatever had been elevated in the tube was. This spectacle stayed in this way for almost a half hour or more.

It was then that the specks we had seen descending were drawn back up to the craft and vanished from our sight. But the other one remained suspended in the middle. The craft then suddenly stopped pulsing and began to glow brightly again with the swirling blue color moving around within it. The entire lake area and the countryside below it was glowing again and it started to move. Slowly it was gliding silently over the lake and heading virtually directly for us. Not a word was being spoken among those who remained. To a person we were awestruck and silent. Each of us staring in utter amazement. It must have been a football field away and coming closer. I could now see that this was in fact a glowing structure. It had a definitive shape and form and its shape was most definitely that of a large disk which had to be 400 feet wide and not 200 feet as I had originally thought. It was enormous. The shaft of blue light remained totally intact and unmoving as the ship itself moved over the lake. The ship was now maybe 150 feet above the lake and the shaft filled the void between it and the surface of the water.

It was then that the water started to chop up just like it would on a windy day. But it was only choppy within the confines of where the light tube contacted the lakes surface. Everything else was still calm around its perimeter. The light was drawing on and or disturbing the water as it passed over it. And now I could see beyond the shadow of doubt that what was lifted from the earth into the light tube was a gigantic Bigfoot. It looked like it was in a state of suspended animation. Being held in the light some 75 feet off the lakes surface. It didn't move an inch and was completely aglow in the soft blue light. The saucer passed by us just to our east with the edge of the craft going right over our heads. We all just kind of turned like automatons watching it going away when suddenly there was a bright flash of light and it was all over. The disk was totally and completely gone. Not flying away at a high rate of speed. It had just vanished in a flash. We all just stood there for a few moments. I think I speak for everyone when I say that we were in a daze. It was almost as if we had been taken over by some type of force while this whole thing had unfolded before our eyes. Seeing the Bigfoot motionless within the tube of light was unbelievable to say the least. And what the connection was between it and the craft is unknown to all of us. We simply saw what we saw when we saw it. And we are talking about nearly 20 people at the start of it all. And more than likely a dozen when it ended. I mean that's allot of witnesses to anything.

This actually happened and we were there to testify of it happening. Now to stand in the open country in total darkness and watch this massive silent glowing and pulsating disc moving across the landscape was intimidating. I mean we all know jets and prop planes. Ultralights and rockets and the like. But to behold something 400 feet in diameter moving at a snail's pace and hovering motionless at times. While not so much as making a sound was mind-blowing. It had to be some type of inexhaustible energy source. The brightness of all of the lights. The continuous pulsing and glowing.

I mean think about it. When we fly on a jetliner there are the cabin lights and a few lights on the fuselage of the jet. This entire craft was a light. And it contained numerous other tremendously powerful lights within it as well. But you couldn't tell where anything came from. The shaft which appeared below it had just appeared. It wasn't like a big floodlight bulb was seen. There was no shaft and then there was a shaft. The searchlights would come on and then they would go off. The entire skin or covering of this thing was moving. At least that's the way it appeared to our eyes. It was like liquid contained within some type of casing. Moving plasma shifting and melting and swirling together like a big blender of light. Well, well, well my readers. Bigfoot and spaceships. They saw what they saw when they saw it is what the man just said. And who am I to argue. Just like I saw the snowy owl and you didn't. That was one jaw dropping account in anyone's book. It just so happens to be in mine.

✗

The Black Bear Incident

The following account was told to me by a guide named Chase Redmond. Here is what chase had to say. As you already know I am a hunter who offers my guide services as well to paying customers. Unfortunately as a guide this means exposing some of our best areas for hunting to the public. Let's face it if someone is ponying up several thousand dollars to hunt with me. I have an obligation to put my best effort forth in order for them to get what they came for. And this means exposing my best hunting areas to total strangers. The area that I am about to talk about is one such place. All that I am willing to tell you is that the location is near the shore in the Pacific Northwest. This is my absolute favorite site for black bear hunting and it is a former logging site located in the coastal hills. When you enter into this location there are still many logging roads which are well worn and easily accessible by four wheeler. So you can get very deep into the region and move around rather easily by truck scoping out your hunt.

There is one area in particular that looks like an atomic bomb went off. One's first thought would be that the loggers really messed this place up but good. But the reality is that the locations appearance is actually the result of a massive land slide. So large was this event that it dragged entire trees right down to the shoreline. It is an incredible sight to see the power of nature and what can happen as a result of it unleashing its fury. It is my general habit to enter in here and scope from the truck seeking out active bears. Then I will park and move out on foot to continue the hunt. Now it's not that I want to give up any of my trade secrets because I am not really giving up anything at all. Everyone worth their salt who hunts black bear knows that they mark their territories by snapping off tree tops. And it's because of this that I actually came across Bigfoot. I already told you that there are many logging roads still available for use here. But many others are so grown in from the side that they are impassable unless you are on foot. And the bears make good use of these.

I have scored many bears walking right down such trails. And it is when they are walking down these trails that they reach up grabbing some low brush trees and snapping the tops down. I know you are more than likely already saying what does this have to do with Bigfoot? Well the average bear in these parts is between say 4 or 5 hundred pounds. And when they stand reaching up to snap a tree the visible breaks are somewhere in the neighborhood of 6 or 7 feet off the ground. And depending on the freshness of the break. It can be a very good indicator of what has been frequenting any trail in particular. It's a simple enough tool in my bag of tricks. The trails in here are extremely hard packed. So I typically will not see any hardcore tracks. But I will find pad prints which are just superficially seen on the loose surface soil. Prints which may be at best ¼ inch deep. I was alone on this day going into the area in preparation for a hunt the following week with a paid client. My habit was to save some time and try to narrow down the best locations to find our mark. Yes the clients know that they are hunting and there are no guarantees. But as a guide you are not going to get many recalls or recommendations if you don't produce. The clients want to at the very least see what they came for. And if they miss the shot it's not my fault. I had been walking some of the trails examining trees breaks of which there were many. And I had also been using my binoculars scoping out many bears that were in the area.

I think at this time I will attempt to give you a picture of this area where the landslide had occurred. Visually you are seeing a river of tree trunks and branches. Piled one upon another just like the old game called Pick up Sticks when you first dumped them out onto the table. And the bears actually can navigate over and through this mess of timber with great agility. There are literally hundreds of creatures which have made this tangled maze their home. Now let me get back to the trails for a moment. So I was walking the trails looking for tree snaps when I ran across a break that was well out of my reach. Now I can easily reach to seven feet which is most definitely an indicator of a large boar in the area. But I came across a break that must have been 16 feet from the ground. It was actually a smaller tree as opposed to a younger growing sapling if that makes any sense. This tree had a very viable trunk of maybe 3 or 4 inches in diameter and was by no means easy to bend over. The typical bushes or small trees that the bears snap are maybe 2 inches thick at the most. Easily able to be bent down and broken by a bear.

The tree that I was looking at was fresh and viable. And it had been twisted and broken at like I said about 16 feet from the ground. Now think about this for a moment. I am an experienced hunter within the confines of an area that I know very well. I have spent hundreds and hundreds of hours in here tracking and hunting bear using this methodology. I do not suddenly see this break and think that there is a 14 foot tall black bear running around in here. It is an impossibility. And no man had come in here to climb a skinny tree and mangle the top of it for fun. So like any person would do I stood there wondering in my mind just what could have reached to that height and broken it. And for what reason. The next day I had come back in looking for some additional bears in the area. And once again as I was walking one of the trails there was yet another tree break just like the other I had seen. This break was also was very high from the ground. So now I had found two. This was now a pattern and not an accident. To me it seemed as though something was mimicking what the bears were doing. Kind of like you break your trees and I will break mine. At least that's what my mind was thinking at the time.

When you ride on the old logging roads here you are looking down and over the area that was logged. The entire area is now filled with new growth. And when you get down into that new growth you are now meandering around in a sea of small trees and bushes. Ranging in height from maybe a foot to 20 feet tall. It is dense and impassable for the most part. In a hundred years it will have thinned out to a certain degree but for now it is a jungle. And it is extremely easy to stumble across a bear in there. And for that reason most of my clients are very uneasy following me through this brush. But where I lead they will follow. So having seen some bear from my elevated position I had come down into the brush looking for evidence of where they were travelling. I came across some fresh scat and a number of tree breaks. And I now knew the trail they were frequenting. When I got back up to the truck I was about to leave but decided to spend a little more time looking around with my glasses. From my position by the side of the truck I was now looking down and over this sea of trees that I had just been walking around in and describing to you. It was then that I noticed some of the trees kind of wagging around and moving. A sure indication that something was walking through them.

This however is never seen with a bear from this position for they are far too low to the ground. The only time you do see them is on the trail, in the open brush, or when they are climbing on the log piles. This was not a bear. I then started to see some flashes of color. Black to dark reddish brown appearing and disappearing as whatever this was continued moving through the trees. Now mind you I just told you that the trees in the area were between a foot and 20 feet tall. Most of them being between say 8 and 14 feet or so. Whatever it was that I was seeing had to be clearing that height at times for me to lay eyes on it. I could see it was steadily moving parting trees out of its way as it did so. My hope was that I would soon see it because it was heading directly for the river of logs. At that point it would either have to stop and retreat or climb up onto the pile which is exactly what the bears do. I watched intently as it approached the proverbial end of the road and suddenly there it was. Climbing up onto the logs was a huge Bigfoot. The creature started walking around on the pile as though it was looking for something inside of the logs. Occasionally crouching down and reaching inside of the heap.

Every now and then after reaching in I would see it put its hand to its mouth. So it was obvious to me that it was getting some type of food from within the maze of fallen trees. I knew personally from just being around the logs. That there were birds' nests, mice and all kinds of critters that had made this maze of wood their home. But it's beyond me what this Bigfoot was actually eating. It did look to me like it was very familiar with what it was doing. And I was wondering why I had never seen it before or the high tree breaks I had seen earlier. The thought came to me that it had recently moved in and was letting the bears know it was around. Who knows what if any interaction there may be between the other animals and them? It is most definitely a mystery. The creature maneuvered with great dexterity around the logs like a child on the monkey bars and I was looking right at it openly with my binoculars. The fur was long and shaggy and now that it was in the open sunlight it appeared to be slightly blondish red in color with darker undertones.

I would have to say that from my vantage point and having seen glimpses of it going through the trees. That is was close to if not 12 feet tall. At one point I noticed a black bear coming up onto the trees maybe 100 yards away from the beast. As the bear casually came up onto the pile it froze. Apparently being unaware of the giant visitor's presence prior to doing so. The bear quickly climbed back down and scampered away. That gave me immediate feedback as to who the boss is. This bear didn't want anything to do with the Bigfoot. At one point when I was looking directly at his face. I think that it either saw me or perhaps the sun reflecting off my binoculars. Whatever the case was the beast stopped what it was doing and climbed back down out of sight retreating once again into the trees. I was able to see a little color after a few minutes and wondered if it had just ducked into the cover to observe me. Perhaps 10 minutes or so had passed when I could see the trees and brush shaking again indicating it was moving on. I watched this pattern of movement for several hundred yards until it had reached a hillside that was more exposed and open. I saw the creature emerge from the dense brush and walk in the open until it was completely out of sight. At that point it must have easily been 1500 yards or more away from my position.

Going into the future hunting here. Which by the way I still do. I have never seen it again. I still encounter some high tree breaks which to me indicates that it is still around. My feeling is that it really doesn't want anything to do with me or you. I know there is plenty of food around here because of the ongoing dense bear population. We hunt many bear in here and for every one we take there is another to take its place in the food chain. Now I know you want to hear about the details. Most of which I am sure that you have heard before. It had to have been 4 feet wide at the mid-section and at the shoulders maybe 6 feet. Which is very hard to absorb mentally I know. These creatures are totally out of the box when it comes to human comprehension. I am sure it is like when someone first comes face to face with a Bengal tiger or a large crocodile. You are immediately overwhelmed by how big they really are up close and personal. I saw a croc in Africa once on a hunt that was 6 feet wide at the middle and 25 feet long. Seeing this Bigfoot was that type of encounter. It is a once in a lifetime event if that in my opinion. Think about it for a moment. How many of the 6 billion people on earth have seen a 25 foot long crocodile?

And how many do you think will see a 12 foot tall Bigfoot? To me it's all the same. It's simply a matter of time and chance. This thing exhibited great dexterity on the log pile. Its balance and ability to maneuver in and around the logs was amazing. And it appeared to be very comfortable doing so. You and I would be stumbling and trying not to fall. But this Bigfoot was walking around on a random pile of broken limbs and shattered trees like it was no chore at all. It was truly remarkable in every sense of the word. And the way it was able to walk through this dense woodland for long distances as though it was crossing a field of wheat. The shear strength and stamina of these beasts is off the charts. When I had the glasses on it and we were face to face for a moment in time. I could see that its lower jaw was very wide. And I could tell that a fair amount of its face which was darkly colored had no hair on it. As far as its leg, arm and back muscles. Just visualize a large humans and multiply it times twenty. Absolutely enormous in every sense of the word. His upper arm looked like a bull's thigh in my field glasses. One of these could likely pick the tail end of a car up with ease. And the size of its feet in my estimation added to its great balance and ability to walk amongst the logs. At no point did it appear to lose balance or stumble in anyway. It was amazing to see in every sense of the word.

X

The Turkey Hunters Sighting

This account came to me from Danny Rodriguez. A turkey hunter working the western Pennsylvania woods. Here is Danny's story. There are 3 of us who get together every turkey season on a property in Pennsylvania. I have been hunting here for about 12 or 13 years. We pay the landowner a nominal fee to be there and typically we throw him a nice bird at the hunts end. His property is a large tract of land abutting another family's farm. All in all we are likely talking about 300 acres in total. Both of these parcels are against a semi mountainous area comprised of mostly heavily wooded hills and some low lying fields which are predominantly made up of low grasses and some patches of scrubby brush. This gentlemen's parcel was partially farmland at one time. But the area which we hunt in is mostly more of the rolling hills that are patched with deep wheat like grass, trees and some open areas of green grass. The bottom line being that we keep coming back because we never go home empty from this location. On our first mornings set up in 1999. We had positioned ourselves with our backs against the trees in the usual manner. Facing a field where we had very good success the previous year. We began our calls and had heard a numbers of birds responding. After about maybe an hour or so a couple of nice toms started to enter the field following some hens. And moments later my friend Jimmy had bagged our first bird of the trip. This is a premier location and we regularly see fox, deer, groundhogs and quite a few rabbits whenever we are here.

After the first shots are taken you are pretty much out of luck for the day. Unless you are game to come back in the later part of the afternoon. I must mention to you that the Real Tree camo which all of us use. Is just about as perfect a match for this lands tree cover as you can imagine. If you didn't know that we were there I guarantee you that you would walk right by us and never know that we were sitting next to you. That's how perfect the blend is against this bark and cover. We are virtually invisible. The reason why I say this will become clearer in a little bit. The second morning in we had set up as the day before. Our habit was to spread out in somewhat of a line. Each of us selecting the largest tree or grouping of trees we could find to lean against. We get ourselves all comfortable and the calling and waiting begins. On this particular morning there was a heavy damp mist or fog laying in this valley. Our visibility being severely diminished. My recollection is that we could see fairly well for maybe 60 yards or less. Now typically one guy was labeled the caller. It's never a good idea to have several men calling all over the place and stepping on each other's calls.

Doing so in my opinion completely destroys the realism of what you are trying to create. On this morning I was doing the calling. We had heard a number of birds after having spent quite some time calling. And then everything had come to a standstill. This is not all that unusual when you are turkey hunting but in this location it is. We had been batting a thousand here for a dozen years and when we called they came. Now whether or not they would come in range for a shot is another story all together. But they would most of the time at the very least come into view. But this day however the responses had stopped. While we were lying in wait the fog was thickening. The forecast was for heavy rain later in the day but for now our visibility had dropped to maybe 40 yards or less and it seemed like it was going to continue to close in on us. I kept calling periodically and we heard nothing. So we sat still and waited. It's rare but sometimes you don't get much of a response and they will still come in. It was about 7:30 with this misty fog closing in on our hide when I noticed what I will describe as a shadowy figure moving in the boundaries of what we could see and what we couldn't see. Just in the fringe of our visibility at the time.

If it had moved 3 feet further away it would have been completely obscured by the fog. But I saw it and I am sure the other guys did as well. My thought initially was that it was a big guy in a Ghillie suit. Because the silhouette of the figure was so enormous. There was however nobody else authorized by the owner to be where we were. Which is not to say that some loose cannon type of dude could not or would not be running around out here. But he could have been shot. Moments later whatever it was had been totally obscured from view by the fog. And no sooner had that happened then it came stepping right out of the fog in my direction like an actor emerging from behind the stages curtain. It looked like a magician walking through a cloud of smoke. I mean poof and here it came walking right at me. I am sure that the boys saw it and a fear came over me that I can't describe. Of course I had my 12 gauge and it was loaded and ready. But at such a quick notice looking at something about which I was uncertain. I couldn't just drop the gun and shoot. At this point in time whatever it was had reached about 30 yards and closing when I said… Hey man! What the hell do you think you're doing? I could see in my peripheral vision the others guys getting to their feet. All of this happening in maybe 10 seconds. Well this thing let out a loud roar or growl like a pissed off lion and ran into the fog. I mean it turned and took maybe 3 or 4 fast strides and vanished. The other guys ran over and said what the hell was that?

It was just as I blurted out the question to what I thought was a dude. That its face had come into focus. It happened virtually simultaneously to my asking the question. It was not a man at all. It was a Bigfoot. I knew immediately but I couldn't retrieve my words. For prior to that it looked like a big dude in a really thick camo suit. There was no detail to see. But in the last step or two as I was talking the face had come into full view. I could see large black eyes and a big mouth. When it roared there were large square teeth that I could see its mouth now being wide open. Its face was ancient looking and partially covered in hair. The skin looking very weathered and worn. As it roared it kind of twisted its head around at the same time it was moving its arms. I guess it was pissed off but I wondered if this movement helped it to roar. The guys moved over quickly with their guns at the ready. We all knew this was a monster not a stray hunter. This Bigfoot had to be at least 7 feet tall and maybe 4 feet wide. And I could see that its hair or fur was really long like that of a Shetland pony. And as it came closer there was a distinct rotten smell that didn't quite register at the time.

The smell was more than likely being held down by the fog for there was absolutely no wind whatsoever. Maybe two seconds after it roared it turned and disappeared into the fog with a few fast steps. It had huge furry feet which actually had left loads of impressions in the field. And we could see in the grass after it had left exactly where it had come from and where it had gone. None of us were willing to go looking for this thing in the fog or on a clear day for that matter. I was just glad it hadn't attacked because the quickness with which it had moved away showed me that it could have been on me in a split second. Why I'm not even sure my 12 could have stopped it. That's how big and thick this creature was. I was frightened like I have never been in my life. I remember distinctly that my body was actually trembling as it ran away. As we made our way back to the owner's house each of us were continually looking over our shoulders wondering if we were going to be rushed by this thing out of the fog. When we made it to the house the owner was amazed at our tale. He said that there had always been stories and rumors of such creatures in the state. But never had he ever seen anything himself. These types of things were always spoken about in private circles for fear of what others might think. It was certainly a day that none of us will soon forget.

✗

The Shape Shifter Encounter

Ernest Smitgowski got a little more than he bargained for while on a routine sales trip to Spokane. I invite you to follow along as Ernest spins his fantastic tale. I was in Spokane Washington on a routine sales trip in the summer of 2004. I was then and still am now employed by a major electronics distribution firm having a number of clients and prospects in the region.

This was a four day trip which typically involves a little wining and dining depending on the client and their wishes. My habit is to also get in some running or hiking time if I can plug it into my schedule wherever I may find myself. I had been here many times before and there are some fantastic areas to hike. Many of which are quite challenging. A fair amount of my clients are younger and game for just about anything. And I have hiked, skied and fished with more than a few of them. But this day I had no takers so I was going it alone on the Quartz Mountain Lookout Trail. I was told that there were some fantastic views of the surrounding area at the top of this trail after having reached the fire lookout station. Now as I begin I must tell you that this isn't called Quartz Mountain for nothing. It is in fact predominantly made up of quartz. And in the world of the paranormal quartz and limestone are said to be engines for weird and strange occurrences.

I mention this now because what I am about to unveil to you and your readers is out of this world strange. So I began my days hike up to the fire tower. There are actually a number of trails that one can take depending on the level of difficulty which you are willing or unwilling to endure. I chose the prior. The first ¾ of the hike was relatively speaking uneventful. It was the last ¼ where the trails start to tighten up and are closely flanked by allot of hanging branches and woods. I had made it to the top and climbed up into the fire tower to have a look see and grab a bite. From this point I could see four lakes. Spirit, Hauser, Newman and Liberty to be exact. At the time I didn't know their names having learned them later on. I was looking around with my binoculars checking out the lay of the land when my eyes locked on to something white moving around on a grassy field that was nestled in the trees below me. And I do mean below. This field was very far from where I was. It appeared to be a small girl wearing a white drees with no shoes on. She was spinning around and running about in this field like any other small child would having fun.

I watched her for almost 20 minutes as she frolicked around in this field. I kept saying to myself that at any moment someone would come into the field to get her. Such as an adult mother or father. I mean she couldn't be out here alone. And if so was she lost? You could imagine the thoughts that were running through my mind as

I stood watching her in the distance but nobody else came into the field. Finally my fatherly instincts kicked in and I decided that I had to go down and try to locate her. What if she was really lost or something. She could die out here and nobody would know. There was no way that I could walk away from here today without knowing she was alright. So I estimated the distance she was away and what trail would best take me to her and I departed. Now once you're in the trails and trees none of which I was seeing was now available for the viewing. It was a blind hike downhill in what I hoped was the direction I would find the grassy field and the girl. When I tell you that I was moving fast I am not kidding. A strong sense of urgency had welled up within me about this little girl. I was going down the slope at a frantic pace hoping that at any moment the forest would break open revealing the field. And after about 30 minutes it did.

I broke out into the field and immediately started to look in every direction for the small child and I didn't see her anywhere. My immediate thoughts were that this maybe another field which possibly had been closer to my position at the top. A field that was obscured from my view by the forest below and the angle of the mountains slope. So I figured I would keep going across this field and continue in the direction I was heading. When suddenly I heard what sounded like a little girl singing. It was very faint. I stopped and started to look around in every direction. And there standing well out in the field was the little girl. I couldn't understand it. I had just looked very thoroughly in that direction and saw nothing and yet there she was. Now understand me please. There was nothing in this field to hide behind. And she was now dancing around where she hadn't been only moments before being some 2 or 3 hundred yards away from the nearest woods. So she couldn't have just run out there in a matter of seconds. I stood there questioning my own sanity. Finally I shouted out little girl are you lost? And she didn't respond at all. She just kept skipping and dancing and singing. And I shouted again this time very loudly. Hey there! Little girl are you alright?

Suddenly she stopped dancing standing with her back to me. My hair is actually standing up as I am telling you this because what happens next is out of this world strange. This little girl wearing a white flowing dress and no shoes is now maybe 80 to 100 yards away from me having stopped after me shouting to her. But she is not looking at me and she is standing motionless in the grass with her back to me. When suddenly she starts to transform or change before my very eyes. The dress seemed to melt away as her form grew tall and dark. I wanted to run but I was frozen where I stood. The little girl had changed before my very eyes into a tremendous hair covered monster. I remember grabbing the sides of my head and falling to the ground. I was thinking that I had stroked or something terrible and that I was going to die out here. I was just lying there in the grass holding my head and thinking. Trying to sort out the pieces of what was happening. I rolled onto my side and sat up. I was looking around and trying to regain my composure when my eyes locked onto this creature that had been the little girl. I sat there and I watched as this monster walked away crossing the entire field disappearing into the trees. I am not quite sure how long I sat there. I was alone and couldn't come to grips with what had just happened. At some point I made it to my feet and began making my way back to my car.

That afternoon I found myself walking into a doctor's office. As I was sitting in the waiting room I wasn't even sure of what I was going to say. I thought I had lost my mind momentarily in that field. But how could that be? I had been watching the girl from the top of the mountain and then found her when I came down the mountain. I was eventually called in and the doctor came in asking me what he could help me with. After I had spun my yarn in a somewhat rapid fashion. He told me that the mind can do funny things. He asked me if I had been working long hours and travelling allot. I knew he thought I was off my rocker and more than likely popping some pills. And frankly I couldn't blame him. Who would believe such a story? And so the doctor gave me a script for something to help me sleep telling me to follow up with my regular doctor when I got back home. To this day I cannot shake the events of that afternoon and it haunts me like a reoccurring nightmare. Well my dear readers. There you have it. Yet another incredible testimonial from a man who had absolutely nothing to gain by telling his story to me or you. A well-spoken, energetic and well educated man. The father of three in his mid-forties. Who finds himself trapped suddenly going about his normal day. Trapped between reality and what? And therein is the true question. What is it that people are seeing and experiencing? For the whole world cannot have gone simply mad. Or can they?

✗

A Message From the Author

My dear readers. As long as I have breathe in my body and the ability to do so. I will continue to bring these sightings and evidential findings to your eyes in future volumes of Bigfoot Terror in the Woods Sightings and Encounters. With that being said expect the unexpected both in my books and in your life. For you may very well be the next witness to Bigfoot…To be continued.

X